GOLD MEDAL
RESCUES

The first gold medal rescue. Commander Charles Fremantle RN swims out with a line to a Swedish
brig. The brig is pounding the sea-bed with every passing wave.
(The full story of the rescue appears on page 4.)

The Arranmore lifeboat, K.T.J.S., takes off a survivor by breeches buoy from the sinking Stolwijk. The lifeboat crew were awarded medals from the Dutch Royal Family for this rescue.
(The full story of the rescue appears on page 4.)

GOLD MEDAL
RESCUES

Paintings by
Tim Thompson

Text by
Edward Wake-Walker

David & Charles

RESCUE FROM A SWEDISH BRIG
Christchurch, Hampshire, 8 March 1824
(Illustration, page 1)

The first gold medal for bravery followed an incident only four days after the founding of the RNLI. Commander Charles Fremantle RN, employed by HM Coastguard at Lymington, was the first to react to the plight of a Swedish brig which had been driven broadside on to the shore at Christchurch, when he plunged into the surf with a line around him. The ship, her mainmast over the side, was in imminent danger of breaking up as her hull pounded the bottom.

The intrepid commander swam to the wreck and managed to get her boats cut clear, only to see them immediately filled by the heavy seas. Unable to persuade the brig's crew to act on any of his other suggested means of rescue, he re-entered the water and was hauled back to the shore by the line, arriving exhausted and unconscious on the beach. When the ship began to break up, her crew were fortunate enough to reach shore using the fallen mainmast.

Fremantle, later Admiral Sir Charles Fremantle GCB, continued an illustrious career, taking charge of transports and shipping in Balaclava Harbour during the Crimean War, then commanding the Channel Fleet, and finally becoming commander-in-chief at Devonport. Most enduringly, however, he gave his name to the western Australian town of Fremantle when, as commander of the frigate *Challenger*, he took possession of the west coast of the continent on behalf of the Crown in 1829.

THE *STOLWIJK*
Wrecked off Arranmore, Co Donegal, 7 December 1940
(Illustration, page 2)

A hurricane from the north-north-west had driven the 3,500-ton Dutch steamer *Stolwijk* onto a reef three miles to the south of Tory Island, which lies off the Donegal coast. Early attempts to rescue her crew had ended in disaster, as the captain and three crewmen of a destroyer had lost their lives trying to reach the stricken ship in atrocious conditions. Then ten of the steamer's crew were drowned when the ship's boat was smashed to pieces in a desperate attempt at escape.

Arranmore's lifeboat, *K.T.J.S.*, under the command of Coxswain John Boyle, had fought her way through mountainous seas and snowstorms for more than five hours to reach the wreck, where the eighteen remaining crewmen huddled near the stern. Every breaking sea swamped them and threatened to wash them away for ever. The lifeboat anchored and veered down on the wreck, and by a miracle, the first line she fired at the *Stolwijk* was seized by the crew and a breeches buoy was rigged. As the lifeboat plunged and swung on her cable, five men were hauled aboard by the rescuers.

Then the line, chafing against the steamer's side, parted and the coxswain had to use all his skill to avoid the rocks and the casualty herself before successfully hauling up the anchor, repositioning and getting another line to the remaining survivors. Ten more soaking men were dragged to safety, but again the line parted – and again another was rigged between the two vessels. The last three men were taken aboard the lifeboat four hours after the rescue operation began; and then it took five more hours of steaming through the unabated hurricane to land the survivors at Burtonport on the mainland. Coxswain John Boyle received the gold medal for this prolonged demonstration of courage.

Copyright © Text and illustrations: Edward Wake-Walker 1992
© Paintings: Tim Thompson 1992

The right of Edward Wake-Walker and Tim Thompson to be identified as authors of this work has been asserted by them in accordance with the Copyright, Designs and Patents Act 1988.

A catalogue record for this book
is available from the British Library

ISBN 0 7153 9900 4

Typeset by Icon Exeter, Devon
and printed in Singapore by CS Graphics Pte Ltd
for David & Charles   Brunel House   Newton Abbot   Devon

CONTENTS

A Commendation from HM The Queen Mother, *Patron of the RNLI* · 7
Artist's Preface · 8
Introduction · 10
RNLI Gold Medal Awards for Gallantry · 93
Acknowledgements and Bibliography · 95
Index · 96

RESCUES DEPICTED IN THE MAJOR PAINTINGS

1 The *Admiral Berkeley, Portsmouth, 1824*	*14*	
2 The Loss of the Yacht *Fanny, Jersey, 1825*	*18*	
3 Rescue from the Steamer *St George, Douglas, 1830*	*23*	
4 The Loss of the *Scotia, Mid-Atlantic, 1839*	*28*	
5 Wreck of the Steam Packet *Thames, Isles of Scilly, 1841*	*30*	
6 The *Royal Charter* Tragedy, *Moelfre, 1859*	*34*	
7 The *Indian Chief, The Goodwins, 1881*	*38*	
8 The *Harold, Anglesey, 1908*	*42*	
9 The *Rohilla* Rescue, *Whitby, 1914*	*46*	
10 The Wreck of the *SS Fernebo, Cromer, 1917*	*50*	
11 The Daunt Rock Lightship Rescue, *Ballycotton, 1936*	*54*	
12 Rescue from the Trawler *Gurth, Humber, 1940*	*58*	
13 The Canadian Frigate *Chebogue, Port Talbot Bar, 1944*	*64*	
14 The Yacht *Maurice Georges, St Helier, 1949*	*67*	
15 The Wreck of the *Hindlea, Moelfre, 1959*	*70*	
16 Rescue from the *Johan Collett, Guernsey, 1963*	*74*	
17 The Loss of the *Lyrma, Start Point, 1976*	*77*	
18 The *Revi* Rescue, *Off the Humber, 1979*	*80*	
19 The *Bonita, Mid-Channel, 1981*	*84*	
20 The Penlee Tragedy, *1981*	*88*	

RESCUES DEPICTED IN THE VIGNETTES

Rescue from a Swedish Brig, *Christchurch, 1824*	*1*	
The *Stolwijk, Arranmore, 1940*	*2*	
The *Claire, Isle of Wight, 1838*	*6*	
The *Alice, Arbroath, 1827*	*20*	
Rescue from *La Constance, Hastings, 1830*	*21*	
The Wreck of the *Good Intent, Formby, 1833*	*27*	
Rescue from the *New Commercial, Cape Cornwall, 1851*	*33*	
The *SS Browning, Ballyquintin, 1942*	*62*	
Rescue from the *Runswick, Peterhead, 1942*	*63*	
The *John and Jessie, Holy Island, 1825*	*92*	

THE *CLAIRE*
Aground at Brook, Isle of Wight, 29 November 1838

The French brig *Claire* was en route from Marseilles to Honfleur when a gale carried her into Freshwater Bay off the Isle of Wight. Soon after daybreak she ran aground some three cables from the shore off Brook. She lay there at the height of the gale, the seas making a clear breach over her. The nine-man crew took to the rigging.

Lt Henry Symmes RN, a coastguard officer, made three unsuccessful attempts to reach the wreck with a line fired by rocket apparatus, then abandoned his efforts. Instead, he grabbed a boat which had been washed ashore from the *Claire*, and with four men put out into the surf. With the brig about to sink, her master and two seamen were hauled into the boat. The lieutenant could take no more survivors for fear of sinking, and headed back, but not before securing a line to the wreck and carrying it with him to the shore.

Before they reached the beach a heavy sea swamped the boat, but her eight occupants were saved by two men who rushed into the surf. Furthermore, thanks entirely to the rope communication with the shore, the remaining six men on the wreck reached safety shortly before she went to pieces. Lt Symmes received the gold medal.

As the remaining crew look on from the rigging the Claire's *boat is upset and all occupants thrown into the sea. They are soon rescued by the shore party.*

In the fifty-five years during which I have been Patron of the Royal National Lifeboat Institution I have maintained a high regard for a service which is ever on call and whose members are ready to face the dangers of a stormy sea to save life.

I remember so many occasions when I have attended RNLI functions: some, like the dedication of the Memorial to the Longhope crew, and the presentation of medals for gallantry have filled me with a sense of pride and admiration; while others, such as when I have been asked to name a new boat, have been happy events which have enabled me to meet many people connected with the Institution. The latest naming ceremony, at Thurso, gave me particular pleasure as the boat, with my name, operates in the Pentland Firth, whose waters I look out on from The Castle of Mey.

I commend this book to all those who appreciate selfless devotion and courage, whether or not they themselves have experience of the sea and its moods.

Elizabeth R
Queen Mother   *1992*

Her Majesty Queen Elizabeth the Queen Mother meets the retired Coxswain Thomas James King on 30 May 1975, the day she visited St Helier, Jersey to name the town's new lifeboat after him. Thomas King was awarded the RNLI's gold medal after he rescued the crew of the French yacht Maurice Georges *in September 1949 (see page 67 for the full story). (Photograph by courtesy of Jersey Evening Post.)*

ARTIST'S PREFACE

Van de Putte Studios

As a description of sea conditions the words 'Snarling mountains of fury' are sufficient to inspire anyone to paint. They were used by Cox'n Dick Evans when he gave me his account of the *Hindlea* rescue for which, in 1959, he was awarded the RNLI gold medal for conspicuous gallantry. He is now a grand old man, and to this day he cannot understand how he managed to extricate himself, his crew and those he rescued from that 'boiling cauldron of foam'. He explained to my mother and me (my mother accompanied me on my visit to Anglesey) over lunch in his captivating Welsh accent, 'my little lifeboat was at one moment flat on her side with mast under water, the next falling stern first off the coaster's deck.

Then I gained control, only to find myself thrown under her thrashing propeller.' His narrative brimmed with detail, but the time comes when a marine artist has to ask such questions as 'What was the colour of sea and sky?' 'How was the superstructure and hull of the *Hindlea* painted?' All went well, but as I planned a painting showing the lifeboat under the thrashing propeller, I needed to know even more detail, and so I asked, 'Dick, was the *Hindlea* fouled with any particular weed or barnacles?' To which he replied after a moment's thought, 'Well, do you know Tim, I don't think I had time to look.' I decided to paint Dick's rescue broadside on, showing a snarling mountain at the bow and another having broken, thundering toward the rocks, with the lifeboat near *Hindlea*'s bridge, her crew about to pluck a seaman to safety, with the ship 'yawing' at her single anchor chain.

Before leaving Moelfre, having paid a fond farewell to Dick and Nancy Evans, I went just a few hundred yards west of where Dick had fought his great battle in 1959, to where, a century before, the *Royal Charter* met her end. Standing on those slabs where so many poor men, women and children had been dashed to pieces was, to make an understatement, eerie. It was dusk, a chill wet fog was manifesting itself and the sea, though silent, rendered a malevolent, haunting tableau. There were 459 casualties. The superhuman efforts of the people of Moelfre saved 41 men. Without the people of Moelfre, few if any would have survived.

My very first paintings of storm-tossed seas were inspired by my father's tales of our deep-sea fishing forbears of Hull – stories of amusing escapes from impoundment by Icelandic gunboats, getting 'Iced in', and coming home many weeks late to read their own obituaries in the *Hull Daily Mail*. Also, sadly, of being lost at sea.

My Great Uncle Frank was the youngest trawler skipper in Hull, receiving his Master's Ticket at the age of 21. He was highly successful, but whilst trawling off Iceland during a storm, a huge wave swept him to oblivion, complete with his wheelhouse and bridge. He had received many medals for lifesaving and was a very strong swimmer, but in such violent weather all his resourcefulness, including hanging on to the log line, was to no avail and he was lost. Later, in World War I, his brother Henry was tragically killed when the minesweeper on which he was stationed mysteriously blew up.

My grandfather, last in the family line of professional mariners, had his Steam Hopper cut in two by an outwardbound trawler. Luckily, on impact, all hands were aft and they leapt on to the trawler as their vessel quickly settled. Then, to the consternation of all, grandfather was seen springing back aboard the now 'awash' aft half, calling out 'Me bike, me bike!' as he dashed nimbly to the funnel, to which he had strapped his brand new bicycle. As the aft half of the hopper submerged, so he stepped from the rail aboard the trawler once more, one hand for himself and one for his much-cherished bicycle.

This anecdote brings me neatly on to Henry Blogg of Cromer, known as 'the greatest lifeboatman of them all'. He seemed to have a predilection for casualties that had become segregated fore from aft, and many a joke was made at his expense – that the prerequisite for him to attend a rescue was that the casualty must be in two parts.

When I painted the pictures for this book, I had to peel back veils of spray, rain and snow to make the subjects visible, falsifying somewhat the true scene, which would have been almost imperceptible for more than seconds at a time. As for example, in the *Royal Charter* gale where, as well as being lashed with spray, stones and seaweed, witnesses recorded being rolled up the fields by the pure force of the wind.

I was delighted when Edward Wake-Walker, Public Relations Officer of the RNLI, offered to write the script for the book. I had previously read some of his pieces and was relishing the alliance. He is a charming and eloquent chap, always ready to help despite the immense pressure of his workload. We selected jointly which gold medal rescues we were to portray. It eventually involved the painting of over thirty rescues, showing as many aspects of these special services as possible. We required oared, sail, steam, petrol, and diesel lifeboats, from the earliest cobles, to the Aruns of the 1980s. To include the varied and diverse casualties, we needed yachts, bulk carriers, light vessels and frigates, etc., and we also wanted to include rescues from Scotland, Wales, Northern and Southern Ireland, and England.

We found that most of the rescues had very scant detail; in fact all I could find on one particular gold medal rescue was 'He swam out with a rope.' The task became enormously frustrating as I was not able to commence a picture without a vital bit of information. Sometimes things as major as how many masts had fallen at the time of the rescue, or what the time of day was when she struck were not known. Worse still, on the meagre information I had gleaned on one picture, after months of research I decided to go ahead and 'paint and be damned', and was promptly damned as a letter arrived turning my light into darkness. This letter proved conclusively that I had painted the scene at the wrong time of day.

The selection of rescues ended in the pursuit of more daytime rescues. However, the more we researched, the more the sun sank. So many of the chosen few golds were night-time services. More horrible still, the masts and sails I have so much enjoyed painting in the past were commonly overboard and torn to rags. Some vessels rescued at sea were mere hulks, dead in the water and totally dismasted. Was our book going to be 'sparless and bible black?' It was then that I thought I would probably be forgiven for 'throwing a little light' on my darkest hours, however contrived. And so, for example, I brought the moon out for Gammon's *Chebogue* service and Hubert Petit's rescue of the *Johan Collett*, also using lightning where necessary.

The most harrowing painting that had to be done was that of the *Solomon Browne*, rescuing the crew of the *Union Star*, the most recent and memorable of the gold medal rescues. I wanted to show the moment Cox'n Trevelyan Richards and his crew had successfully saved four of the coaster's people. This is a positive feature of this rescue, and one that I hope will not be the cause of any distress to the bereaved families, the sensibilities of whom I was constantly mindful, even though eleven years have passed since that dreadful night.

TIM THOMPSON

A lugger similar to La Constance *(page 22) becalmed in St Helier Harbour, near Elizabeth Castle. The yacht* Fanny *(page 18) was wrecked just outside this harbour.*

INTRODUCTION

In the 169 years of the Royal National Lifeboat Institution's existence, only 118 gold medals for gallantry have been awarded. That in itself is a measure of how jealously the Institution guards the honour, reserving it for acts of bravery in circumstances beyond the worst nightmares of most seafarers. If anything, too, it is becoming more difficult to win gold, only thirty-three having been awarded since the beginning of this century and only nine since the last war.

THE ROYAL NATIONAL LIFEBOAT INSTITUTION
Past and Present

The RNLI of the 1990s, judged purely by its boats and equipment, is scarcely recognisable from the 'Shipwreck Institution' founded by Sir William Hillary back in 1824. Today there are well over two hundred lifeboat stations operating high-powered craft of every size from 16 to 54ft. They answer some 5,000 calls a year and save about 1,500 lives in the process.

Search and rescue cover can now be guaranteed up to fifty miles off the coast in all weathers around virtually the entire coast of Great Britain and Ireland. Modern electronics have revolutionised the business of locating casualties and navigating in hostile conditions. Modern boat design and engineering have given lifeboat crews protection and manoeuvrability their forebears could not have contemplated. By the end of 1993 even the celebrated lifeboat shape – a craft pointed at both ends – will no longer be in use. By then the RNLI will have fast lifeboats at every station.

And yet remarkably, in its constitution and its volunteer spirit, the Institution has kept very closely to the original blueprint drawn up by Sir William Hillary all those years ago.

As a thriving mercantile nation of the eighteenth and nineteenth centuries, Britain had come to accept that shipwreck was an occupational hazard, the unwelcome partner of commercial success. Indeed, Lloyds of London can be said to have risen to prominence through the unpredictable nature of the weather and the sea. Gentlemen in the City had developed an efficient system to reduce the risks of financial ruin to those whose ships and cargoes were threatened. Until the turn of the nineteenth century, however, very little progress had been made in providing similar safeguards to the sailors whose lives were constantly at risk.

Even if the repercussions of terrible loss of life from a shipwreck were not severely felt in the City, it was generally a different story on the coast. To see a ship wrecked within a few hundred yards of where you live, to see people drowning before your very eyes and to be powerless to help is a bitter experience and was depressingly frequent for coastal inhabitants two hundred years ago.

Records show that as early as the 1770s some local people made attempts to provide a means of rescue. In Formby, Lancashire a boat was stationed among the sand dunes specifically for helping shipwrecked sailors on that part of the coast. A little later, in 1786, the Crewe Trust at Bamburgh, Northumberland, bought a rescue boat. The Trust was a life-saving service which for fourteen years had been sending out horseback patrols during storms to look for ships in trouble. The boat they acquired could well be described as the first lifeboat; it was the special design of the coachbuilder and inventor, Lionel Lukin, who had converted a fishing boat to make it as he termed 'unimmergible'.

The awakening of a more widespread will to offer hope to the seafarer in distress came after a tragedy in the mouth of the Tyne in 1789. A group of Newcastle businessmen was so distressed after witnessing the drowning of all aboard the wrecked *Adventure* in a storm that they arranged a competition to find

THE LIFE-BELT IN USE BY THE CREWS OF THE LIFE-BOATS OF THE NATIONAL LIFE-BOAT INSTITUTION.

The requisite qualities of a life-boatman's life-belt are—

1. Sufficient extra buoyancy to support a man heavily clothed, with his head and shoulders above the water, and to enable him to support another person besides himself.

2. Perfect flexibility, so as to readily conform to the shape of the wearer.

3. A division into two zones, an upper and lower, so that between the two it may be secured tightly round the waist; for in no other manner can it be confined sufficiently close and secure round the body without such pressure over the chest and ribs as to materially affect the free action of the lungs, impede the muscular movement of the chest and arms, and thereby diminish the power of endurance of fatigue, which, in rowing-boats, is a matter of vital importance.

4. Strength, durability, and non-liability to injury.

The cork life-belt of the NATIONAL LIFE-BOAT INSTITUTION possesses the first two qualities in a greater degree than any other life-belt, and the third one exclusively. (*Vide* annexed figure.)

The Lifeboat *journal, first published in 1852, and received by some 200,000 today, must be one of the oldest house journals in existence. In its early days it saw its role as a teacher, as well as a reporter, of lifesaving and RNLI methods. This 1883 description of the cork lifejacket is an example of its practical nature.*

the best plan of a rescue boat capable of surviving conditions which had prevented any rescue attempt to the *Adventure*.

Some rancour followed the result of the competition when the winner, William Wouldhave, was only offered half the two-guinea prize money (which he contemptuously refused). His tin model which suggested a design which would neither sink, go to pieces, nor lie bottom-up was given to one Henry Greathead, an unsuccessful entrant and local boat-builder, to produce in full-scale reality, incorporating the best features.

The resulting lifeboat, not self-righting but still unsinkable, which came to be known as 'the original', rapidly proved herself and, along with improved successors, acted as a catalyst in the formation of a national lifeboat service. Now that a boat existed which gave sufficient confidence to rescuers to take on heavy surf and high winds, local societies were being formed to operate one.

Lloyds, now showing laudable interest, funded fourteen Greathead boats and were responsible for encouraging the formation of locally run lifeboat stations around the coast. In 1802 Douglas on the Isle of Man acquired its own lifeboat. Here, an eccentric baronet who loved adventure became a member of the crew. In Sir William Hillary there was at last someone who had direct experience of the horrors of shipwreck and who also carried influence with those who counted in the Establishment.

In 1823 he published a pamphlet which proposed a National Institution for the Preservation of Life from Shipwreck. The following year, with the support of MPs, the Archbishop of Canterbury, the Lord Mayor of London and others, a lifeboat service relying wholly on voluntary contributions and volunteer crews came into being.

After the initial impetus and optimism of the first year of the Institution when twelve new boats were bought and permission was given to add the 'Royal' prefix to the title, support began to wane. Annual receipts which were close on a handsome £10,000 in 1825 dwindled over the next two decades until by the late 1840s they were at a bare few hundred pounds. Institution lifeboats became

neglected and unseaworthy and the idea of a national lifeboat service paid for out of voluntary funds appeared to be unworkable.

Ironically it was another Tyneside tragedy which revitalised the Institution. All but four out of the twenty-four-man crew of the locally run South Shields lifeboat were lost when she capsized attending a wreck in the mouth of the Tyne on 4 December 1849. This disaster aroused much public attention and sympathy and the following year inspired the fourth Duke of Northumberland to offer a hundred-guinea prize for the best new model of a lifeboat, echoing the exercise of sixty years earlier.

By 1851 a winner had been announced. His name was James Beeching and although a few lifeboats were built to his plans, the committee judging the

The RNLI of the 1990s operates all-weather lifeboats capable of 18 knots, and can guarantee search and rescue cover up to fifty miles off the coast. This is the 47ft slipway-launched Tyne class lifeboat stationed at Selsey in Sussex.

competition recommended some modifications. They asked James Peake, one of their members, to incorporate what was best from all the models submitted. The result was a 30ft self-righting lifeboat which formed the basis of the RNLI fleet for the next fifty years.

In the same year the Duke of Northumberland was appointed President of the Institution. Thanks to his influence and to the energies of a bright young barrister, Richard Lewis, who had recently been appointed Secretary, the fortunes of the Institution were turned round and new boats and equipment began to appear again on the coast.

In order to climb out of its parlous financial state, the RNLI was forced in 1854 to accept an annual grant from the government. As the situation improved the grant became more of an impediment than an advantage with its attendant government conditions. An unaided organisation also seemed more attractive to voluntary supporters and it was therefore with considerable satisfaction that the Institution regained its independence from state support in 1869. To this day that status has remained the same.

THE RNLI GOLD MEDAL

When the RNLI was founded it had a dual purpose. Not only did it set out to provide the means of rescuing people from shipwreck, it wanted to reward those prepared to carry out the task. In this way Sir William Hillary sought to encourage others. Much of the early Committee of Management's business was deliberating over who should receive what in terms of rewards for rescues. The first few chapters of this book will give an impression of how decisions were reached (not without controversy) but clearly in those early days class distinctions told.

The officers got the medals, on the whole, and the men the money. Not bad money, it must be said; a reward of three sovereigns after a gold medal rescue would have been several weeks' wages for an impoverished fisherman. The medals themselves were highly prized too. Sir William Hillary himself had no qualms about ensuring that his Committee was well appraised of his many adventures aboard the Douglas lifeboat. He did not always agree with their decisions but nonetheless ended his days with four gold medals, three for bravery and one for founding the RNLI.

How brave do you have to be nowadays to receive the RNLI gold medal? It is known by some as the lifeboatman's VC. Certainly this book contains examples of courage and disregard for personal safety in every way equal to the most outstanding acts of bravery on the battlefield. Nowadays, in its official guidelines the RNLI's criteria for a gold medal award reads simply: 'The gold medal will be recommended for a rescue which has been effected as the result of an act in which outstanding courage, skill and initiative has been shown.' The silver medal is awarded for acts similarly described but which 'just fall short of the standard required for the gold medal'; likewise the bronze's relationship to the silver.

Not much to go on, one might argue. In reality, though, a very careful system is employed. When the regular report of a rescue reaches RNLI headquarters and it is clear it is one out of the ordinary, the report is sent to the relevant divisional

From 1882 to 1939 the RNLI maintained a depot at Poplar in London's East End. This illustration was engraved soon after its opening. Spare lifeboats and transporters were kept there, men worked in a rigging loft, and a crane was used to haul boats out of the water and to test them for self-righting.

inspector of lifeboats to investigate. He will then submit a fuller account of the incident to the Institution's director with a recommendation for a reward if he sees fit. The director will endorse or amend the recommendation and submit it to the Executive Committee of the RNLI. If a medal is mooted, particularly a gold, the committee will go to great lengths to ensure that comparisons are made with earlier medal rescues to ensure that they are not devaluing the currency of the award.

A book about a handful of gold medal rescues cannot, of course, portray the RNLI past and present in its intricate entirety. The service is as much about patience and dedication as it is about outstanding heroism. Lives are more often saved because the lifeboat got there in time than because the coxswain risked his neck and those of his crew to reach a casualty. But it is only historic incidents such as the *Indian Chief* rescue, the wreck of the *Rohilla* and the heroic reputations of Hillary, Blogg and Evans which have given the RNLI its unique place in the hearts of the public.

Agonising decisions have been taken about which rescues to feature in this book. Inevitably not all have happy endings, notably, the wreck of the *Royal Charter* and the tragedy of Penlee in 1981. But without these stories, a true picture of the dangers of the sea would not be shown.

As this book goes to press eleven years have already elapsed since a gold medal was won. There have been silver medals awarded to several stations in that time, some of which have come extremely close to gold. Not one of those silver medallists, however, nor any lifeboat crew-member, is likely to be hoping to be the next to win a gold. They can imagine the hell which has to be endured to qualify. But it does not stop them from volunteering for the next call-out, whatever it might bring.

The
GOLD MEDAL RESCUES

1

THE WRECK OF THE *ADMIRAL BERKELEY*

Portsmouth, 23 November 1824

Gold Medals to Thomas Peake and Samuel Grandy

In the very early days, much of the business of the weekly Committee of Management meetings of the Royal National Institution for the Preservation of Life from Shipwreck was the appraisal of rescues reported to them from around the British Isles.

One such rescue took place on 23 November 1824, barely nine months after the Shipwreck Institution's foundation, when the 290-ton transport ship, the *Admiral Berkeley*, was wrecked off Portsmouth in a storm. She had been on passage to Cape Coast Castle in South Africa and was carrying 195 people.

Imagine the meeting room at the Institution's original headquarters at 12 Austin Friars in the heart of the City of London. Half a dozen serious gentlemen sit round a table with the City of London's MP, Thomas Wilson, one of the Institution's most influential founding fathers, in the chair. The story of the wreck of the *Admiral Berkeley* and the miraculous rescue of every one of those 195 people is unfolded to them in a series of letters tabled for their attention over a period between 26 January 1825 and 3 August of the same year.

Here extracts of the minutes of their meetings take up the story:

January 26 1825
Read a letter from:

Berkeley but that from a letter they had received from Captain Peake he (from delicacy probably) does not mention himself as having taken an active part; and to request that they would be pleased to favour the Committee with any particular information he could give on the subject.

February 9 1825
Read letters from:

Captain Denning of the *Admiral Berkeley*, from Lt Cheeseman and Lt Saunders respecting the landing of the crew and troops from that ship when she was wrecked at Portsmouth; by which it appears that a hawser was conveyed to the shore by one of the seamen of the ship, who reached the shore by one of the ship's masts. That Captain Peake RN was extremely active and deserved the best thanks of every person concerned.

Among the several gentlemen who rendered assistance was Lt Grandy RN who, at the risk of his life, crossed from Portsmouth to Haslar in a six-oared boat; his intention was to have carried the boat across the beach and boarded the vessel, but it was impossible to do so. He however afforded the greatest assistance in landing the troops, baggage, etc, and did not finally leave the ship during the night until after the gale. He contributed the most of any in getting the troops and baggage safe on shore and deserves the highest palm that can be given him. Of his crew, Torrible and Godfrey are particularized as being very useful.

Captain Peake RN, Gosport, in which he mentions that on 23 November his attention was called to a ship, the *Admiral Berkeley*, in a truly alarming and perilous situation, having on board a large detachment of troops, and that from the great exertions of Lt Grandy RN, assisted by Torrible and Godfrey belonging to the Blockhouse crews, is to be attributed in a great degree the safety of the troops on board that ship. [Both Captain Peake and Lt Grandy were officers of HM Coastguard.]

The Secretary was desired to address a letter to the Transport Office to say the Committee had been informed the officers and some of the men of the Coastguard had been instrumental by their exertions in saving the lives of the troops from the *Admiral*

RESOLVED:
That the gold medallion be awarded to Lt Grandy for the very meritorious and gallant manner in which he exerted himself on the occasion; and 5 sovereigns to be by him distributed to his boat's crew.

March 2 1825
Read a letter from:
Lt Clarributt RN and Mr George Mottley, Agent, dated Haslar, 24 February in reference to the case of the *Admiral Berkeley* in which they state that at the time the ship was driven

The Admiral Berkeley aground.
Festing and Walker stand by in their whaleboat after their earlier exertions.

on shore at 8am the situation of the crew and troops was then and long afterwards one of uncommon peril; for had she filled from the dashing of the sea against the wale, few lives in all human probability would have been saved.

That they observed with admiration the personal exertions of Captain T.L. Peake RN in giving the necessary directions for effecting the escape of the people by the gib-boom [*sic*]; this expedient however was not resorted to as the ship was driven gradually along the beach for about three hours when her masts were cut away.

James Torrible and Thomas Godfrey rushed boldly into the surge and extricated a man from the rigging of the mast who had brought a hawser on shore.

That Captain Peake was for six hours wholly exposed on the beach to the violence of the storm, drenched by the sea and in a stream of water dashing over the causeway which he bore with a degree of patience and perseverance as highly creditable to the honorable service to which he belonged, as to himself individually.

RESOLVED:
That the Gold Medallion be presented to Captain Peake RN and two sovereigns to James Torrible and Thomas Godfrey.

Read a letter from:

Captain G.W. Willis RN of *HMS Brazen*, Spithead, in reference to the *Admiral Berkeley* saying that Lts Festing and Walker, 1st and 2nd Lieutenants of the *Brazen*, were very serviceable in assisting in this case and that the latter with five seamen at the suggestion of Lt Festing manned the whale boat of the *Brazen* and after considerable fatigue and great risk of their lives, succeeded in crossing the harbour's mouth and getting to the *Berkeley* where he met Lt Festing who also then suggested a raft to be made, which with their united exertions was done by their own hands, after which these two officers, assisted by the whale boat's crew succeeded in landing the troops, women, etc.

RESOLVED:
That the Silver Medal be presented to Lt Festing RN and to Lt Walker RN and 5 sovereigns to the men composing the boat's crew.

July 27 1825
Read a letter from:

Lts Festing and Walker of *HMS Brazen* dated 20 July saying they beg to return the two Silver Medals awarded them by the Honorable Society but think it necessary to say that if their exertions do not merit a Gold Medal the equal award of those whose services did not extend beyond the beach until every arrangement had been made by themselves on board the unfortunate *Admiral Berkeley* for the preservation of the lives of the much exhausted men, women and children embarked on board of her, they prefer the award of their own feelings and that of the hundreds of eyewitnesses to the fact.

Ordered that the papers relating to the *Admiral Berkeley* be laid on the table till the next meeting for the inspection of any of the members of the Committee.

August 3 1825
Referred to the note from Lts Festing and Walker dated 20 July.

To write them that the Committee regret to learn they were not satisfied with the Medals they were voted on 2 March last and to say that the Committee came to the vote from the whole of the information that was laid before them at the time.

So ended the committee's deliberations over the wreck of the *Admiral Berkeley,* at least as far as the minute book is concerned. It would appear that they had a difficult task piecing together a variety of reports and learned, if they did not already know, that to single out individual acts of bravery from the chaos of a shipwreck is a perilous task in itself.

LEFT
Peake and Grandy assist the passengers and crew from the stricken ship.

2

THE LOSS OF THE YACHT *FANNY*

Off St Helier, Jersey, 9 January 1825

Gold Medals to the Brothers De St Croix

Sir William Hillary, although its founder, was never Chairman of the 'Shipwreck Institution' as the RNLI first became colloquially known. The original chair was given to one Thomas Wilson MP, whose constituency, the City of London, made him ideally placed regularly to attend the weekly committee meetings in London.

Occasionally, however, Sir William left the Isle of Man where he lived and came to London. At the meeting held on 27 July 1825 he had taken the chair in Thomas Wilson's absence. It was at this meeting that the rescue of survivors from the French yacht *Fanny* was examined for possible awards.

The three De St Croix brothers, Francis, Jean and Philip, must have been men after Sir William Hillary's heart. Islanders like himself, they lived on Jersey and are described in the committee minutes as 'gentlemen of property who keep a boat for the purpose of assisting persons in danger'.

By now thirteen lives had been saved and the rescuers were just about to return for the remaining six people aboard when the *Fanny* suddenly disappeared beneath the waves. Tragically the six drowned, five bodies being recovered soon afterwards and the sixth, that of a little girl, nearly a fortnight later.

The story does not quite end there although scant details mean that some unanswered questions remain. The *Fanny* was apparently refloated a few days later and taken to St Helier. What became of her then is not known. However, by some very strange coincidence, another St Malo registered vessel, also called *Fanny*, was wrecked almost exactly three years later on 1 January 1828 a mile from St Helier harbour. She even had the same master on board, Captain Destouches. Were they, in fact, the same vessel?

The Institution's Committee of Management took the unusual step of awarding the gold medal to each one of the three De St

The three men are reported to have been at a 'convivial party' on the night of 9 January 1825 when at around 6pm they heard a gun fire. Suspecting that it meant someone was in trouble, they left the party in haste and ran to the beach. Sure enough, a yacht, the St Malo registered *Fanny*, was aground on rocks known as Les Buts to the south-west of Elizabeth Castle, not far from Jersey's capital, St Helier.

Without a moment's hesitation they seized the first boat they could find and with three other men, namely Philip Nicolle, Philip John and George Marshall, set out towards the wreck. The weather is described as 'thick and hazy' and there was a dangerous swell. In fact, a pilot boat which had reached the scene earlier was deterred from approaching the yacht when her skipper saw, and probably heard, the heavy surf breaking around and over the vessel on the rocks.

The men in the pulling boat pressed on regardless. They successfully got alongside the sinking yacht, grabbed some of her occupants, pulled away and landed them ashore. They then made a second sortie and again managed to stay alongside the yacht long enough for more people to leap to safety. They, too, were put ashore.

Croix brothers. The remaining three aboard the rescue boat were reported to the committee as being 'persons in a humble sphere of life' and were consequently awarded three sovereigns each for their services.

At a subsequent meeting of the committee a letter was read from the Mayor of Jersey, Edward Nicolle, saying that two of these three men had gratefully received their three sovereigns but that the third, Philip Nicolle, although 'highly sensible of the compliment intended him', declined taking the money 'as pecuniary reward was foreign to his feelings'.

The Mayor added that he was confident Mr Nicolle would, however, highly prize the gold medal 'which would be a stimulus on future occasions, should they unfortunately occur'.

A further letter from the father of the De St Croix brothers was read, beseeching the committee to consider Philip Nicolle for a gold medal and even offering to 'defray any expense attending it.'

The committee wrote back to the Mayor saying they seldom awarded the gold medal, let alone three for the same service, but if Mr Nicolle was prepared to accept the Institution's silver medal, they would send one.

The De St Croix brothers and crew fight their way through heavy surf to the yacht. The detail (left) shows Destouches at the shrouds, frantically signalling for assistance.
In the background is Elizabeth Castle and the Oratory.

RESCUE FROM THE *PROVIDENCE*
Polkerris, Cornwall, 26 August 1826

Prompt and courageous action by coastguard officer Lt John Else RN, meant that the lives of eight men aboard the seine fishing vessel *Providence* were saved when she was driven among rocks outside Polkerris Pier, near Fowey in Cornwall. The eight crewmen were washed overboard, and Lt Else, first ordering the coastguard gig to be manned, took himself and another man out to the wreck in a 14ft punt.

They managed to pull three survivors on board before the punt was driven onto rocks in the heavy surf.

Lt Else was severely injured and could take no further part in the rescue. The punt was recovered, however, and all its occupants saved. The gig was also successful, bringing the remaining five shipwrecked men alive to the shore. The gold medal was awarded to Lt John Else.

Providence is on her beam ends. A heavy sea is running into the rocks, but after prompt action by
Lieutenant Else the rescue of all her eight crew was made possible.

THE *ALICE*
Aground at Arbroath, Fife, 8 March 1827

Lt Christopher Jobson RN, a coastguard officer stationed at Arbroath was the first man to be awarded two gold medals for bravery. Both acts occurred within a month of each other. His second gold medal was won on 8 March 1827, when the vessel *Alice* ran ashore at 2am in a severe gale and snowstorm. The Manby line-throwing apparatus, was carried 300 yards to a position near the wreck: its second shot reached the main boom of the casualty. But her crew could not make use of it and the link slipped into the sea.

With eleven crewmen, Lt Jobson then launched the Arbroath lifeboat and in the turmoil reached the wreck and was able to take off the master.

Sadly, the remaining crewmen were drowned.

Jobson and his men finally reached the Alice. *They rescued the master but the others aboard perished.*

RESCUE FROM *LA CONSTANCE*
Hastings, Sussex, 19–20 January 1830

Overwhelmed in a heavy gale and snowstorm, the French lugger *La Constance* fetched up on the Sussex coast at Fairlight, near Hastings. Ten men and a boy were aboard her and, in the darkness, they despaired of being rescued. However, they had not taken into account the courage of two Royal Navy lieutenants, Horatio James and John Prattent from *HMS Hyperion*, part of the Sussex blockade at the time.

This pair, both of whom would be awarded the gold medal, led a number of coast blockade men into the very heavy surf and rescued the master of the lugger and all of his crew, bearing them on their backs along the coast for three miles, and restored them to consciousness near Fairlight, at Tower Number 3. However, one Frenchman fell victim to the cold and later died.

Showing a blue light to indicate distress, the terrified French seamen despair at their perilous situation.

3

RESCUE FROM THE STEAMER *ST GEORGE*

Douglas, Isle of Man, 20 November 1830

Gold Medals to Sir William Hillary and Lt Robert Robinson

The Royal National Lifeboat Institution had been in existence for six years when its founder, Sir William Hillary, became involved in a rescue which would earn him his third gold medal for gallantry but which would also leave him with injuries from which he never fully recovered.

Hillary was not a Manxman by birth; he retreated to the Isle of Man after he lost most of an inherited Jamaican sugar-plantation fortune raising a regiment to fight the French. His patriotism earned him a baronetcy and little else but he became extremely active in Douglas, not least by involving himself as a regular crew-member aboard the local lifeboat.

It was in 1823 that he wrote his famous appeal to the nation proposing that a countrywide organisation be set up to preserve life from shipwreck. The following year, thanks to the influential contacts he had formed during his earlier existence, he persuaded royalty, archbishops, politicians, naval officers and financiers to join a committee to manage a brand new Royal National Institution for the Preservation of Life from Shipwreck.

The St George Company of Liverpool, which operated most steamship passenger and mail services between the Isle of Man and the mainland, received a shock in 1830. They had a Manx-run rival on their hands in the form of the new and speedy steamer *Mona's Isle*. She was the Islanders' answer to a service which until then had been slow and unreliable.

The spur of competition had forced the Liverpool company to take their flagship, the *St George*, off the Dublin run and to pit her against the Manx ship in a blatant race from Liverpool to Douglas.

In spite of a severe south-westerly gale which swept the Irish Sea on Friday, 19 November 1830, the two vessels set out and arrived the same evening in Douglas Bay after a neck-and-neck race through heavy seas. Both ships were forced to anchor in the bay as the tide was out and they could not enter the harbour. Passengers were ferried ashore by harbour boats along with the mail and other freight.

Lt-Colonel Sir William Hillary Bt, founder of the RNLI in 1824. He lived in Douglas on the Isle of Man and was himself a crew-member in the town's lifeboat. A hero of the St George *rescue, he was awarded no fewer than three RNLI gold medals for gallantry in his time and a fourth for founding the Institution.*

At this point their captains made different decisions. Lieutenant John Tudor RN, in command of the *St George*, resolved to remain at anchor for the night in the comparative shelter provided by Douglas Bay against the south-westerly gale. His rival skipper, William Gill, a Manxman, aboard the *Mona's Isle*, suspected the wind might change to a less favourable quarter and elected to leave the anchorage and head out to sea.

Sure enough, during the night the wind backed south-easterly and increased to a severe gale. The *St George*'s captain had kept steam up all night as a precaution, with the men at their stations. Even so, when the worst happened and the anchor chain parted at about 5am, the captain could not manoeuvre away in time to avoid being driven violently on to St Mary's Rock. Immediately she filled with water, settling down forward and lying broadside to the most jagged part of the rock.

After the initial shock, the crew's first reaction was to attempt to launch a small boat so that some men could get ashore to raise the alarm. They were lucky to escape with their lives. The boat immediately overturned, the men disappeared into the surf but somehow resurfaced long enough to grab lifelines thrown down by their comrades aboard the wreck.

A second attempt to save themselves was made when the captain ordered the foremast to be felled so that it could be used as a raft by which the crew could reach the centre of St Mary's Isle and wait for rescue at daylight. The mast came down but the plan failed and the mast was left trailing over the side of the steamer. The captain had also fired distress flares and now all he and his crew could do was to pray that someone had seen them. His ship could break up at any moment.

The flares had indeed been spotted and in very little time Douglas lifeboat, with the familiar erect figure of Sir William Hillary standing at the stern, was tossing and plunging through the darkness towards the wreck. Sir William at sixty was not the oldest man aboard the lifeboat. His faithful coxswain, Isaac Vondy, was five years his senior. One supposes that there were younger men among the sixteen volunteers who accompanied them, including one Lt Robert Robinson RN and the local agent for the St George Company, a gentleman named William Corlett.

The crew of the ten-oared 29ft lifeboat, *True Blue*, pulled manfully until they were in a position to let go their anchor to windward and veer down towards the wreck. But the surf breaking around the reef nearly swamped the lifeboat and it was all that her crew could do to pull her clear and prevent disaster.

Hillary knew that there was one other possible means of getting near. With the tide as it was and with the lifeboat's shallow draught there was in theory enough sea covering the rocks on which the steamer had foundered for the lifeboat to make an approach between her and the higher rocks of St Mary's Isle. However, to ensure an easy exit the lifeboat would need to reverse into the position. The fallen mast was acting as a barrier which meant there was only one way in or out.

Although it was for his own salvation, Lt Tudor aboard the steamer was horrified when he realised what the lifeboat was about to attempt and he screamed to the lifeboat crew to pull back. He was convinced they were on a suicidal mission. Sir William ignored him and against all the odds his crew brought the lifeboat into the gap amid the boiling and very shallow sea.

She was now in the greatest of danger. Huge seas rolled into the blind alley the lifeboat had entered and with each one the lifeboat suffered new damage. Her rudder was torn away, six of her ten oars were either snapped or lost overboard, and some of her airtight cases were stove in.

Then one massive sea roared in and lifted the lifeboat to a near-vertical position. Two boatmen together with William Corlett and Sir William Hillary were hurled into the water. All but the latter were quickly hauled back into the boat. Sir William, who could not swim, felt himself being dragged beneath the surface and then thrown with massive force against the hull of the *St George*. Miraculously a rope from the rigging then fell into his grasp and he hung on, his head barely above the water.

By this time Lt Robinson had somehow transferred to the wreck from the lifeboat and he and Lt Tudor, hanging by lines down the side of the steamer, hauled Sir William from the sea. Six ribs were broken and he was severely bruised.

In spite of his condition he was determined to carry on in command. He realised now that with the lifeboat so badly disabled there was no possibility of her crew hauling her, laden with survivors and against the wind, up to her anchor. The only way out was the passage blocked by the fallen mast.

For two hours the crewmen worked with knives and an axe in a desperate and exhausting effort to clear the mast and rigging. All that time the lifeboat was sustaining yet more damage as she wallowed in her narrow gully of turbulent sea. Several times she was nearly swamped.

At last the men could do no more even though some of the mast and rigging

The True Blue *lifeboat veers down on her cable and, in the narrow channel between the steamer and St Mary's Isle, prepares to take on board the twenty-two imperilled seamen.*

25

A portrait of the veteran Douglas lifeboat coxswain, Isaac Vondy, who accompanied Sir William Hillary on so many of his missions of mercy. Hillary's Tower of Refuge can be seen in the background.

RIGHT: Two years after the wreck of the St George, Sir William Hillary had built this Tower of Refuge in Douglas Bay on the very rocks which were the scene of his famous rescue. The tower was intended to give shelter to anyone wrecked in the bay, that they might scramble there and wait for eventual rescue when the weather had moderated. Wordsworth referred to it in a sonnet of 1833 as: 'Blest work . . . of love and innocence.' It stands to this day with the RNLI flag flying from its turret. (Photograph by courtesy of Roger Oram.)

had not been freed. At enormous risk to shipwrecked and rescuers alike the twenty-two crew of the steamer began to lower themselves into the crippled lifeboat. Some of them carried buckets to help with baling.

Sure enough, the lifeboat began shipping water once all survivors were aboard and the men baled furiously as others prepared to make the exit. By now huge waves were breaking over the wreck and one, just as the lifeboat was edging her way through the tangled barrier, lifted her and then let her fall crashing onto the edge of St Mary's Isle.

Immediately she was caught by another breaker and all but capsized. Her occupants were thrown about but managed to stay aboard by clinging to ropes. It remained for one man to cut a retaining line which had been fastened between the wreck and the lifeboat's stern.

When this was done the lifeboat was at last washed clear of the wreck and was carried by a wave coming round the bow of the *St George* which left her in calm water on the sheltered side of St Mary's Isle. Two harbour boats were now making their way from Douglas having seen the plight of the lifeboat. One of them was able to take some of the survivors off the lifeboat while the other passed a tow-line aboard and was able to beach the lifeboat and allow her occupants to gain dry land.

Not one life had been lost during the entire episode. While Sir William Hillary received his third gold medal for bravery (he actually held a fourth for his part in founding the RNLI), Lt Robert Robinson was also awarded the gold medal and Isaac Vondy and William Corlett received silver medals.

THE WRECK OF THE *GOOD INTENT*
Formby, Lancashire, 29 November 1833

Pilot Boat No 1 of Liverpool, the *Good Intent*, was being driven before a November storm towards the Lancashire coast with a number of pilots aboard, when her punt was washed off its stowage on the deck and tore into the belly of the sail. With her canvas in shreds the pilot boat was unmanageable, and soon drove onto Formby beach.

In fact thirteen men on board were drowned; nevertheless as the wreck settled, a surgeon by the name of Richard Sumner, watching from the shore, became determined to go out and offer help to anyone left alive. Judging that no boat could get near, Mr Sumner stripped off his clothes and, armed with nothing more than a bottle of rum tied round his neck, entered the icy water and swam to the wreck. Hauling himself onto the deck he found eight men and a boy still alive. First he administered the bottle's contents to the survivors, then brought them all safely to the beach where, finally, he used his medical skills to revive them. He was presented with the gold medal for bravery; a very just reward.

Sumner, with his rum bottle tied around his neck, climbs aboard the Good Intent. *He then administered its contents to the shipwrecked men and assisted with their transfer to the shore.*

4
THE LOSS OF THE *SCOTIA*

Mid-Atlantic, 5 December 1839

Gold Medal to Captain John Collins, Master of the US Ship Roscius

It is tempting at first to question Captain John Collins' gold medal after his ship picked up the survivors from the ill-fated *Scotia* in mid-Atlantic on 5 December 1839. On the face of it, the greatest risk he took was a commercial one. By stopping his sailing passenger-ship *Roscius* to give help and by forfeiting a fair wind, he was in danger of being overtaken by a steam-driven trans-Atlantic rival.

However this was December, the sea was very rough, a gale was threatening, darkness was falling and anything including financial ruin could have befallen the captain and his ship as he waited to carry out the rescue.

The *Scotia*, a ship of 600 tons, was out of Quebec and bound for Glasgow with a cargo of timber when the weather got the better of her. The *Roscius* came upon her on the afternoon of 5 December. Seeing distress signals, Captain Collins altered course and when near enough to hail her he was told that she was waterlogged with 17ft of water in the hold.

A passenger aboard the *Roscius* gave his own account of what happened when he came ashore at Liverpool nine days later:

The Roscius *rides a heavy sea as a boat approaches from* Scotia.

every moment of importance. We had, moreover, 70 steerage passengers and 21 in the cabin; and to forego taking advantage of a fair wind and to lay to for a night in a heavy sea, with every appearance of an approaching gale, was a determination which, I greatly fear, many a master of a ship would have found difficulty in coming to.

'Captain Collins, however, made this resolution prompt, and without any expression of impatience at the detention it occasioned. His only observation was: "We must stay by the poor devils at all events till morning, we can't leave them to perish there, d——n it."'

Much to everyone's relief, no doubt, the all-night wait did not prove necessary. Captain Jeans of the *Scotia* managed to launch his ship's boats a little while after Captain Collins made his gallant resolution. Through the gloom and heavy seas all twenty-four men on board were safely transported to the side of the *Roscius*, a passage which had taken the best part of an hour to complete. The passenger concludes:

'The prompt reply of Captain Collins was: "Put out your boats if you want to come on board." A cheer from the people of the sinking vessel followed, and the thrilling cry arose as of men in the extremest peril suddenly restored to life and hope. Every person was instantly on the poop.'

The *Roscius* now made an attempt to near the *Scotia*. The waterlogged ship was quite out of control, however, and pitched heavily as the seas swept over her. The poop deck was, in fact, the only safe place left to her crew. As the two vessels began to close, the *Scotia* staggered down upon the *Roscius* whose captain was forced to make sail to get out of the way.

In the very heavy seas, the *Roscius* lay to about a mile from the *Scotia*. The passenger's account continues:

'It is impossible sufficiently to commend the conduct of Captain Collins; his anxiety to reach Liverpool before the steamer which was to have sailed six days after us, made

'To the credit of the master of the *Scotia*, he was the last man to leave the sinking ship. The anxiety expressed by the men in the first boat for the safety of the captain... showed how highly he was respected and esteemed by his crew, and, if he had not been so, he would probably not have kept his ship afloat so long as he had done.

'Nor was the anxiety of Captain Jeans for the safety of his crew less manifest: the first question he asked on coming on board the *Roscius* was, "Are all my people safe?" The captain and crew were all Scotch and their conduct throughout reflected no discredit on their country. The men had been night and day at the pumps since the previous Tuesday and exhausted as they were, they turned to and did duty with our crew.

'And no sooner were the boats cast adrift than there was ample occasion for their services. A violent gale from the north-east set in, which must have rendered it utterly impossible for the people to have taken to their boats and the violence of which on the following day must have been inevitably fatal, for it would have been impossible to have kept the pumps going. The sea already, even before the gale set in, was making a clear breach over her, and threatening to carry away her poop cabin.'

The waterlogged ship Scotia *wallows in the Atlantic swell. Captain Collins holds* Roscius *hove to, as the boats bring the* Scotia's *people to his vessel.*

29

5

THE WRECK OF
THE STEAM PACKET *THAMES*

Isles of Scilly, 4 January 1841

Gold Medal to Captain Charles Steel RN

*Captain Grey orders that the women be handed down into the boat,
whilst Mr Morris bids a fond farewell to his daughter Cecilia from
the cabin window.*

The story of the wreck of the steam packet *Thames* is undeniably one of tragedy and of gallantry. However, it is unfortunately unclear from RNLI records precisely why Captain Charles Steel RN was singled out for a gold medal when so many Scillonian men were involved in the desperate attempt to rescue the crew and passengers.

It is known, however, that a lifeboat of the RNLI was only stationed at St Mary's thanks to the insistence of the good captain. He was the inspecting commander of the Coastguard on the Islands at the time and when the rescue took place had at his disposal one of the Institution's Pellew Plenty standard designs, a 26ft, ten-oared, sixteen-year-old lifeboat.

In those early days of the RNLI it would appear that the islanders were still inclined towards their more familiar off-island gigs than an imported lifeboat when it came to entrusting their lives to the mercy of an Atlantic gale in their shoal-strewn waters. Therefore, when blue lights of distress were spotted close to Jacky's Rock to the south-west of the Islands on the morning of 4 January 1841, three gigs were the first to launch, the *Thomas*, the *Bee* and the *Briton* from St Agnes. The pilot cutter, *Active*, from the same island, had to wait a while for the tide to float her before she, too, could set out to the rescue.

Meanwhile at St Mary's, Captain Steel was using all means of encouragement and persuasion at his disposal to muster a crew for his lifeboat, which had not until that moment been tested in anger. At first only four men came forward: two coastguards, a seaman and a local labourer. Eventually, enough men to pull the ten oars were cajoled aboard and the lifeboat set out, like the gigs, battling against massive seas and freezing squalls of hail and sleet.

The 500-ton *Thames* had been on passage from Dublin to London with thirty-five passengers and twenty-six crew aboard when she was hit by a severe westerly gale and very heavy seas. With the treacherous Brow of Pond's Reef off the Isles of Scilly immediately to the east, she became disabled when seas found their way below decks and extinguished the boiler fires. She was at the mercy of the storm and all aboard soon felt a sickening lurch as she struck Jacky's Rock.

The steam packet Thames, *driven onto the Brow of Ponds Reef, begins to sink by the bows.* Bee *and*
Briton *gigs and* Active *cutter await a lull as the* Thomas *gig goes to the rescue.*

31

The gig *Thomas* reached the scene first and by some miracle and superhuman feat of strength by her crew got close enough to the wreck to catch a line. The men then hauled themselves under the steamer's weather quarter, ready to receive survivors.

The steamer's captain, James Grey, ordered that the women be sent down first. One young woman by the name of Cecilia Morris was seized by the rescuers, having been reluctantly released by her father. Two stewardesses, Mary Meyler and Mary Gregory, were next but before they could be lowered down to the gig, a wave filled the small boat. In spite of this mishap the two women were dragged through the sea and hauled aboard.

Fate then intervened. A sudden squall whipped up the waves and the gig began to plunge and toss with such uncontrolled fury that her crew could no longer maintain their hold alongside the stricken ship. They had to pull back and join the other rescue vessels which were sheltering under the barely adequate lee of Gorregan.

The three women, soaked and shivering, were transferred to the pilot cutter which had a small cuddy in her bows and which gave them some protection. Determined to save the lives of at least these three, all now showing signs of severe exposure, her skipper then decided to take them back to St Agnes without further delay. The women were put ashore at 3pm.

The other rescue boats waited and waited near the wreck hoping for a lull in the weather. None came. On board the *Thames* twenty young army recruits in desperation set about launching the two ship's boats. They were all drowned in the attempt.

Then the sailors lashed together makeshift rafts and as the main mast crashed down, tearing up the decks and causing the wreck finally to disintegrate, the remaining survivors floated off. The unfortunate souls were not to last long. The rafts were soon overturned by the waves with some of the people being dashed ashore on the island of Rosevear. Some may well still have been alive at this point but only one was to survive the night on the rocks. He, a seaman by the name of Edward Kearson, found himself a cask which he stuffed with grass and in which he spent the night.

The rescue party remained steadfastly at sea all night, forced to wait until daybreak before the rocks of Rosevear could be searched. Kearson they found alive. He confirmed their worst fears that no one else was alive on the island. In all, fifty-seven lives were lost in the wreck.

Lifeboat returning.

RESCUE FROM THE *NEW COMMERCIAL*
Cape Cornwall, 11–12 January 1851

The gold medal was awarded to both Captain George Davies RN, of HM Coastguard, and Commander Thomas Forward of the Revenue, following this largely tragic incident off Cape Cornwall, four miles north of Land's End. Four other coastguardsmen and six more Revenue men were also honoured with silver medals.

All eight crew, the master Captain Sanderson and his wife from the 250-ton Whitby brig *New Commercial*, managed to scramble onto a rocky shelf after their vessel had struck the Brisons Rocks in thick fog and high seas and was immediately broken up. But shortly afterwards a huge wave washed them all from their precarious refuge, and only one crewman, the master and his wife found themselves still alive among the rocks. The crewman then showed remarkable resourcefulness by constructing a raft with a sail from the wreckage, and making his way upon it to Sennen Cove where he found help.

Meanwhile the Revenue cutter *Sylvia*, under the command of

Thomas Forward, had been ordered out from Penzance and in terrible conditions launched a boat in an attempt to reach the desperate couple. The task was impossible, and the boat only regained the cutter with utmost difficulty. In the falling darkness the commander hove to for the night, hoping that his close presence overnight would help the two survivors from despairing completely.

By 1pm the next day, with seas marginally less treacherous, five boats had joined the *Sylvia*, one of which contained Captain George Davies and a rocket apparatus. Having ordered his crew into another boat, and risking severe scorching and potential capsize to himself, he fired a line towards the couple. On the second attempt it reached them and the master tied it around his wife's waist. She was pulled through the water just as three immense seas nearly swamped the rescue boats. The master was recovered in a similar fashion and was eventually landed at Sennen. Sadly his wife died before she could be got ashore.

The master of the New Commercial *and his wife pray for salvation, marooned on the Little Brison Rock. Gallant Captain George Davies risks severe scorching and potential capsize as he fires his rocket line. The Revenue cutter* Sylvia *and other boats stand by.*

6

THE *ROYAL CHARTER* TRAGEDY

Moelfre, Anglesey, 26 October 1859

Gold Medal to Joseph Rodgers

This book features two gold medal acts of bravery which took place close to the village of Moelfre in Anglesey. By coincidence, the second rescue took place precisely one hundred years after the first and although both involved a shipwreck, the loss of the *Royal Charter* on 26 October 1859 turned out to be as tragic as the rescue of the crew of the *Hindlea* on 27 October 1959 was triumphant.

This is the terrible story of the wreck of the record-breaking passenger ship *Royal Charter*, the first steam-and-sail-driven liner able to promise passage between Liverpool and Melbourne in under sixty days.

The *Royal Charter* was an iron-built ship of 2,719 registered tons and approximately 320 feet in length. She had three tall clipper masts, a single funnel and an auxiliary 200-horsepower engine designed to take over when the winds were calm or contrary. Speed and luxury (for the first- and second-class passengers, at least) were her main attractions to fare-paying passengers on the Australia run.

Her maiden voyage from Liverpool in 1856 coincided with the height of the Australian gold rush and when the *Royal Charter* left Melbourne on 26 August 1859, under the captaincy of Thomas Taylor and with a crew of more than a hundred, she was crowded with close on four hundred passengers returning home to England, many of whom were families who had amassed a fortune in the gold mines. There was over £300,000 worth of gold in the hold.

By the time the ship had reached Queenstown on Ireland's southern coast, the captain was the toast of his passengers. They were nearly home after an untroubled voyage and Liverpool, so the captain promised, was only twenty-four hours away, a mere fifty-nine days out from Melbourne.

Even as they forged northwards through the Irish Sea with a light but favourable south-east wind and only a ripple on the water, there was no indication whatever of the storm they were about to meet as they turned north-east, then east to round Anglesey. No shipping forecast existed to warn her captain that already a hurricane, the worst in living memory, was wreaking havoc in the south and moving inexorably north. By the time it had left the British Isles the storm had sunk 133 ships, damaged 90 more and claimed 800 lives.

By 6.30 on the evening of 25 October the *Royal Charter* was rounding the Skerries, a group of small islands at the north-west tip of Anglesey. The wind had now strengthened considerably and was blowing from the east. On she steamed almost directly into the wind along the coast of Anglesey, pitching and tossing more and more violently as the seas and wind increased.

The Maltese seaman Joie Rodriguez (better known by his anglicised name Joseph Rodgers), who reached the shore with a rope, thus saving a few precious lives in the tragic wreck of the Royal Charter *in 1859. Somehow he survived in waves breaking sixty feet high against jagged cliffs. This earned him a gold medal.*

The breeches buoy link to the shore was made possible by the daring swim of Joseph Rodgers. The crowd of people on the forward part are holding back, but the riggers seize the opportunity to escape. Other passengers are grasping the ship's rail as hurricane-driven walls of water burst Royal Charter's *iron plates open.*

35

Somewhere between 9 and 10pm Captain Taylor lost control of his ship. The engine could no longer provide headway against the storm (sails were of no use in the head wind), and when the captain attempted to steer northwards away from the rocky shore on his starboard side, the ship would not respond to the helm. Instead, she was being driven rapidly towards the shore by the wind which had now moved round to the north-east and which had reached a murderous hurricane force.

In a final attempt to regain control the captain ordered certain sails to be set and maximum possible steam from the chief engineer to see if he could swing the ship's head right round into the wind. If this were possible he could then set a course which would take him out into the Irish Sea and clear of land.

Three times the ship began to come round and three times the gale forced her back. Unbelievably, the wind was still strengthening. To let go an anchor was the last chance. One hundred fathoms of chain were paid out on her port anchor, but even with the engine turning to reduce the strain the drift could not be entirely checked. Then the starboard anchor was released and fresh hope was felt on board the ship. The captain believed, or at least told his passengers he believed, that he had his ship 'fast by the nose'. This did not prevent him from sending out distress rockets which, even if they had been seen, would not have summoned help in those conditions. No lifeboat could have made it through the surf and the pilot boats already at sea were fighting for their own survival.

At 1.30am on October 26, the strain on the port anchor cable was too great and it parted. An hour later the starboard chain also succumbed and the *Royal Charter* was doomed. Before long every man, woman and child aboard the ship felt the shock of the sea-bed against the iron hull beneath them.

Still the captain tried to quell the growing panic. They were on sand, not rocks, the tide was receding and by daybreak everyone would be able to walk

The brave people of Moelfre risked their lives as they pulled survivors from the surf.

ashore. He was right about the sand but wrong about the rest. The tide was flooding and remorselessly through the night the ship was lifted by the tide and bumped across the sandy bed by the force of the storm towards a lethal rocky headland just to the north-west of the village of Moelfre.

In the night the three huge masts of the *Royal Charter* had been felled by her crew to lessen wind resistance and the vessel's drift, but when dawn broke everyone aboard was staggered to see that they were within twenty-five yards of the jagged rocky ledges of the land. So near and yet so far; a tumultuous sea with waves breaking sixty feet high against the cliffs separated the shipwrecked from the shore. Meanwhile, to seaward mountainous rollers crashed over the vessel as she lay broadside on to them.

While the hull of the ship remained intact there was still a faint hope. Villagers from Moelfre were on the cliffs now, desperately waiting to see how the people on board could save themselves as there was precious little help they could give from the shore. If only a line could be passed ashore from the ship, a bosun's chair could be rigged and people could be hauled to safety one by one.

On board the *Royal Charter* a Maltese seaman whose original name, Joie Rodriguez, had been anglicised to Joseph Rodgers, volunteered to swim ashore with a line tied round his waist. Every crew-member knew that such an act was the only hope but Rodgers was the man prepared to carry it out. His strength and fearlessness had already been tested to their limit throughout the night. During the captain's desperate earlier efforts to manoeuvre out of danger Rodgers had been up and down the mast several times setting sails.

Refusing even a life-jacket, Rodgers lowered himself by a line over the side of the ship and, waiting for the right moment, let the sea take him. His shipmates were sure he was lost, almost from the moment he let himself go. However Rodgers seemed to know what to do. He did not attempt to swim for the shore, merely to stay afloat. He allowed the huge waves to lift him up and carry him forwards and then back again towards the ship. This way he did not need to fight his way through the mass of splintered timber and tangled rigging which heaved in the water all around him.

Eventually the sea deposited him on an abrasive shelf of rock. He fought to keep his hold upon it as the receding wave dragged him angrily back towards the sea. He won the battle with the wave but the next one was now approaching and was bound to swamp him and dash him against the cliff. Three Moelfre men had seen him and came scrambling forward to help. By linking hands in a chain the leading man was able to grab Rodgers and although the next wave arrived and covered them to the waist, they retained a hold and Rodgers was safe.

Within a short while a ten-inch hawser had been passed ashore and made fast to a rock. An escape route existed.

The bosun's chair had been rigged from the bow of the ship and the majority of the passengers were gathered in the stern. To begin with, before they could be brought forward, an unfortunate squabble delayed the use of the bosun's chair for some fifteen vital minutes. A young lady passenger, the girlfriend of the officer in charge of the device, refused through fear to be the first to be sent ashore by it. Some riggers were as keen as she was reluctant to be the first and the result was that nobody went for some time.

The after section of the Royal Charter*'s broken hull shudders under the hammer blows of huge seas.*

While the officer, having given up persuading his girlfriend, turned his attention to organising some seventy women and children who were now on the forecastle waiting to take to the bosun's chair, several riggers rushed forward and were hauled ashore on the hawser. Almost immediately afterwards a huge wave engulfed the forecastle and the officer and all the women and children were washed to their deaths.

That was the beginning of the terrible end. Although a few members of the crew scrambled ashore by the bosun's chair after the first disaster, by now the ship had broken in two. The people in the stern section had no means of escape other than to throw themselves into the sea as the ship began rapidly to disintegrate. Even without the encumbrance of their heavy Victorian garments

and in many cases pockets full of their gold, pathetically grabbed at the last moment, the chances of survival would have been practically non-existent.

A very few did survive instant drowning or being bludgeoned to death on the rocks, but they, along with those who escaped by the hawser, only numbered forty-one. Well over four hundred people died including every officer, every woman and every child on board.

The RNLI recognised Joseph Rodgers' act of bravery by awarding him the gold medal. It was an ironic, if highly appropriate, gesture when one considers how much gold was lost by the passengers (although not by later salvors).

7

THE *INDIAN CHIEF*

Wrecked on the Goodwins, 5 January 1881

Gold Medal for Coxswain Charles Fish of Ramsgate

There will always be new stories to tell of shipwreck and rescue on the Goodwin Sands but the wreck of the *Indian Chief* in the early morning of 5 January 1881 and the rescue performed by Ramsgate lifeboat the following day should never be forgotten. There can be few incidents in the history of the RNLI better recorded (thanks to the journalistic skill of a *Daily Telegraph* correspondent of the day and the descriptive powers of both the mate of the *Indian Chief* and Coxswain Fish himself), but neither will there ever be a more chilling example of the rugged ability to survive of the nineteenth-century seaman.

The facts can be told quite simply: the *Indian Chief*, a 1,238-ton merchant ship, four days out from Middlesbrough and bound for Yokohama, Japan, struck the Long Sands, close to the Knock Light, in an easterly gale at 2.30am on 5 January 1881. Slowly she began to break up throughout the day and when an attempt to launch boats from her only resulted in the loss of two men, the rest of her twenty-nine-man crew made for the rigging. Some lashed themselves to the mizen-mast and some to the foremast. When the main mast fell during the night it brought down the mizen and sixteen men were drowned.

The remaining eleven survived the night in spite of freezing gale-force winds and at first light were astonished to see their salvation approaching through the heavy broken water across the Sands in the shape of Ramsgate lifeboat.

The lifeboat, *Bradford*, a 44ft self-righter, had embarked just after midday the day before under tow from the harbour paddle-steamer *Vulcan*. They had thirty miles to endure in the open lifeboat through the strong biting gale and very heavy seas. Arriving close to the scene in the dark it was impossible to find the wreck. Coxswain and crew then made the brave decision to remain there for the night. The steamer and lifeboat cruised about between the Sands, the lifeboat crew exposed to the whole fury of the storm and the steamer losing her sponsons and sustaining damage to her deck-housing.

In the morning, under her own sail, the lifeboat somehow negotiated the seas around the wreck, drew alongside, took off all remaining survivors, sailed back across the Sands to the *Vulcan* and made it back to Ramsgate after an absence of twenty-six hours.

The gold medal was awarded to her coxswain, and the silver to all the lifeboat's crew and to the master and crew of the *Vulcan*.

Three other lifeboats from Harwich, Clacton and Aldeburgh, also launched to the aid of the *Indian Chief* but, in spite of staying at sea for many hours, were unable to help.

Those are the bare details. The extracts which follow from the mate's and the coxswain's accounts provide the real heart to this story.

The Bradford *surges away from the wreck of the* Indian Chief *with all the survivors aboard. Beyond are the* Sunk *lightvessel, and the paddle steamer* Vulcan *making for deeper water.*

THE MOMENT OF SHIPWRECK

THE MATE: 'Shortly after the Knock Light had hove in sight, the wind shifted to the eastward and brought a squall of rain. We were under all plain sail at the time with the exception of the royals, which were furled, and the mainsail that hung in the buntlines. The Long Sand was to leeward, and finding that we were drifting that way the order was given to put the ship about. It was very dark, the wind breezing up sharper and sharper, and cold as death. The helm was put down, but the main braces fouled, and before they could be cleared the vessel had missed stays and was in irons. We then went to work to wear the ship, but there was much confusion, the vessel heeling over, and all of us knew that the Sands were close aboard. The ship paid off, but at a critical moment the spanker-boom sheet fouled the wheel; still, we managed to get the vessel round, but scarcely were the braces belayed and the ship on the starboard tack, when she struck the ground broadside on. She was a softwood-built ship, and she trembled, sir, as though she would go to pieces at once like a pack of cards. Sheets and halliards were let go, but no man durst venture along. Every moment threatened to bring the spars crashing about us, and the thundering and beating of the canvas made the masts buckle and jump like fishing rods.

THE CREW MAKE FOR THE RIGGING

THE MATE: 'A little before five o'clock in the afternoon a huge sea swept over the vessel, clearing the decks fore and aft and leaving little but the uprights of the deck-houses standing. It was a dreadful sea, but we knew worse was behind it, and that we must climb the rigging if we wanted to prolong our lives. The hold was already full of water, and portions of the deck had been blown out, so that everywhere great yawning gulfs met the eye, with the black water washing almost flush. Some of the men made for the fore-rigging, but the captain shouted to all hands to take to the mizenmast, as that one, in his opinion, was the securest. A number of the men who were scrambling forward returned on hearing the captain sing out, but the rest held on and gained the foretop. Seventeen of us got over the mizentop, and with our knives fell to hacking away at such running gear as we could come at to serve as lashings. None of us touched the mainmast, for we all knew, now the ship had broken her back, that that spar was doomed, and the reason why the captain had called to the men to come aft was because he was afraid that when the mainmast went in it would drag the foremast, that rocked in its step with every move, with it. I was next to the captain in the mizentop,

The stern ornament of the Indian Chief.

Watching the lifeboat from the foretop.

and near him was his brother, a stout-built, handsome young fellow, twenty-two years old, as fine a specimen of the English sailor as ever I was shipmate with. He was calling about him cheerfully, bidding us not to be down-hearted, and telling us to look sharply around for the lifeboats. He helped several of the benumbed men to lash themselves saying encouraging things to them as he made them fast.'

Halfway through that hellish night when each wave tore away another piece of the ship's hull, the mate became convinced on a premonition that he would be safer on the foremast than the mizen:

'So I climbed into the crosstrees, and swung myself on to the stay, so reaching the maintop, and then I scrambled on to the main topmast crosstrees, and went hand over hand down the topmast stay into the foretop. Had I reflected before I left the mizentop, I should not have believed that I had the strength to work my way for'ards like that; my hands felt as if they were skinned and my finger-joints appeared to have no use in them. There were nine or ten men in the foretop, all lashed and huddled together. The mast rocked sharply, and the throbbing of it to the blowing of the great tatters of the canvas was a horrible sensation.'

THE MIZEN FALLS

'Then a great sea fell upon the hull of the ship with a fearful crash; a moment after, the mainmast went. It fell quickly, and, as it fell, it bore down the mizenmast. There was a horrible noise of splintering wood and some piercing cries, and then another great sea swept over the after-deck, and we who were in the foretop looked and saw the stumps of the two masts sticking up from the bottom of the hold, the mizenmast slanting over the bulwarks into the water, and the men lashed to it drowning. There was never a more shocking sight, and the wonder is that some of us who saw it did not go raving mad.'

SALVATION

'When the dawn broke we saw the smoke of a steamer and agreed that it was her light we had seen; but I made nothing of that smoke, and was looking heart-brokenly at the mizenmast and the cluster of drowned men washing about it, when a loud cry made me turn my head, and then I saw a lifeboat under a reefed foresail heading directly for us. It was a sight, sir, to make one crazy with joy, and it put the strength of ten men into every one of us. The boat had to cross the broken water to fetch us, and in my agony of mind I cried out, "She'll never face it! She'll leave us when she sees that water!" for the sea was frightful all to windward of the sand and over it, a tremendous play of broken waters, raging one with another, and making the whole surface resemble a boiling cauldron. Yet they never swerved a hair's breadth. Oh, sir, she was a noble boat! We could see her crew — twelve of them — sitting on the thwarts, all looking our way, motionless as carved figures, and there was not a stir among them as, in an instant, the boat leapt from the crest of a towering sea right into the monstrous broken tumble. The peril of these men, who were risking their lives for ours, made us forget our own situation. Over and over again the boat was buried, but as regularly did she emerge with her crew fixedly looking our way, and their oilskins and the light-coloured side of the boat sparkling in the sunshine, while the coxswain, leaning forward from the helm, watched our ship with a face like iron.'

Summoning the dregs of their energy the survivors unleashed themselves from the rigging and managed to float a line down to the lifeboat, whose crew were able to grab it and haul their craft alongside the wreck. Dodging the waves they scrambled along the remnants of the ship's hull and dropped into the lifeboat.

Coxswain Charles Fish described the rescue just as vividly as the man he saved. The following extracts give some impression of the ordeal and how his crew coped.

'I had my eye on the tug – named the *Vulcan*, sir – when she met the first of the seas, and she was thrown up like a ball, and you could see her starboard paddle revolving in the air high enough for a coach to pass under; and when she struck the hollow she dished a sea over her bows that left only the stern of her showing. We were towing head to wind, and the water was flying over the boat in clouds. Every man of us was soaked to the skin, in spite of our overalls, by the time we had brought the Ramsgate Sands abeam; but there were a good many miles to be gone over before we should fetch the Knock Lightship, and so you see, sir, it was much too early for us to take notice that things were not over and above comfortable.

'I never remember a colder wind. I don't say this because I happened to be out in it. Old Tom Cooper, one of the best boatmen in all England, sir, who made one of our crew, agreed with me that it was more like a flaying machine than a natural gale of wind. The feel of it in the face was like being gnawed by a dog. I only wonder it didn't freeze the tears it fetched to our eyes.

'There was no sign of the wreck, and staring over the edge of the boat, with the spray and the darkness, was like trying to see through the bottom of a well. So we began to talk the matter over, and Tom Cooper says, "We had better stop here and wait for daylight." "I'm for stopping," says Steve Goldsmith, and Bob Penny says "We're here to fetch the wreck, and fetch it we will, if we have to wait a week." "Right," says I; and all hands being agreed — without any fuss, sir, though I dare say most of our hearts were at home, and our wishes alongside our hearths, and the warm fires in them.

'As the seas flew over the boat the water filled the sail that was stretched overhead and bellied it down upon us, and that gave us less room, so that some had to lie flat on their faces; but when this bellying got too bad we'd all get up and make one heave with our backs under the sail, and chuck the water out of it in that way. "Charlie Fish," says Tom Cooper to me, in a grave voice, "what would some of them young gen'lmen as comes to Ramsgate in the summer, and says they'd like to go out in the lifeboat, think of this?" This made me laugh, and then young Tom Cooper votes for another nipper of rum all round.'

Coxswain Charles Fish (bearded, centre) with his crew, pictured following the Indian Chief *rescue.*

8

THE *HAROLD*

Wrecked off Anglesey, 22 February 1908

Gold Medal to Coxswain William Owen, Holyhead

Although steam power had profound influence on rail and sea transport throughout the Industrial Revolution and on into the twentieth century, the use made of it by the RNLI was altogether more limited and more fleeting.

As early as 1824, the same year that the RNLI was established, its founder Sir William Hillary was advocating the construction of a steam-driven lifeboat. It would give the boat, he argued, the great advantage over sail of being able to proceed directly to windward.

Until 1890, however, Sir William's dream boat could not be realised by designers who found combining all the unique prerequisites of a lifeboat with those of a mechanically and steam-driven craft beyond them. Then, in May 1891, the *Duke of Northumberland* began her trials off Harwich. She was 50ft long, of 30 tons displacement, built in steel and fitted with a steam engine. She was driven neither by screw nor paddles, both of which were considered dangerous in a rescue situation, but by a system of water-jet propulsion.

Harold's crew reach for the line thrown from the Duke of Northumberland.

Her trials were undoubtedly successful, she was seaworthy and reliable, and soon she was carrying out rescues in her own right. However, owing to the weight and dimensions of the steam lifeboat, she could not be launched from the shore and needed to be moored in sheltered waters. This limited the number of stations requiring such a vessel and in fact only five more steam lifeboats were built before petrol engines began to be used, soon after the turn of the century, first as auxiliary power aboard sailing lifeboats and then as the main means of propulsion.

In 1897 the *Duke of Northumberland* was moved, after a brief spell at New Brighton, to Holyhead. Here she was to spend the next twenty-five years doing sterling service, being called out 131 times and saving 248 lives.

The most outstanding of these rescues took place on 22 February 1908 when a gale from the west-south-west was causing havoc in the Irish Sea. Coxswain William Owen and his crew had just thankfully regained the safety of Holyhead harbour after an hour and a half at sea assisting the broken-down Liverpool

steamer *Bencroy*. She was aground on the breakwater when the lifeboat got to her but with the help of the lifeboat, which put two men aboard, a tow-line was passed to another vessel and the steamer was towed into the harbour.

A while after 2pm word came that another steamer, the 75-ton *Harold,* was in difficulties. She, too, was a Liverpool ship, owned by Mr T. Best of the Liverpool Lighterage Company. She was carrying a cargo of china clay from Teignmouth in Devon to Runcorn when her engines failed five miles from the coast. She was being driven rapidly by the wind and the ebb tide towards the two rocky westernmost headlands on Holyhead Island, known as the North Stack and the South Stack.

A Barrow steamer, the *Sound Fisher*, noticed her plight and immediately moved in close to try to get a line aboard. Unfortunately the attempt ended in failure but by now the Holyhead lifeboat *Duke of Northumberland* was steaming, for the second time that day, out through the entrance of the harbour.

This time conditions could not have been worse. The wind which was now westerly had increased to an eighty-mile-an-hour hurricane and the waves were monstrous. But, as the *Lifeboat* journal remarked later that year, 'the Steam Lifeboat made headway against it as probably no other boat could have done'.

Meanwhile, the *Harold* had succeeded in dropping two anchors just short of the shore and to the immense relief of her nine-man crew, huddled together on the bridge, they had begun to hold. Earlier the men had attempted to launch the ship's boat but it had been smashed to pieces before anyone could get aboard. Now they could only wait and pray that some form of craft could reach them.

The lifeboat surged onward, lifting and plummeting and rolling in seas that her coxswain had never before experienced. The area of sea around the stricken steamer was yet more ferocious. There was nothing but white, foaming water all around her and the lifeboat, not yet able to get anywhere close, was tossed around like a cork. For two long hours the engineers aboard her, battened down in the stoke-hold, had to endure the almost insufferable motion of the lifeboat

Coxswain William Owen fights to keep his steam lifeboat The Duke of Northumberland *on station. Alongside, the steamer* Harold *is in a perilous situation, embayed and nearly on the rocks.*

43

and maintain power on the engines while their coxswain fought to achieve they knew not what above them.

He had, in fact, all that time been using the limits of his considerable skill to manoeuvre close to the casualty. Each time he came anywhere near, a massive wave would hurl him off course. Finally, as the tide grew slack at low water, he saw his chance. He drove the lifeboat towards the steamer and a crew-member hurled a line at her, which was held.

This allowed a pulley system to be rigged between the two vessels, Coxswain Owen all the while straining to keep the lifeboat in position. He succeeded long enough to allow seven of the *Harold*'s crew to be hauled through the rampaging water to the lifeboat's deck.

What happened next could so easily have meant the end of every man aboard the lifeboat and the casualty. A sea much larger even than any of those preceding it caught the lifeboat and bore her swiftly but carelessly straight towards the *Harold*. Before he could take any effective action, Coxswain Owen found himself alongside the casualty. A foot or two further and the two vessels would have been smashed to pieces.

As it was, with immense skill and presence of mind, the coxswain regained control and with audacious opportunism held the position in which the sea had placed him just long enough for the two remaining survivors to leap aboard the lifeboat.

He then ordered the rope between the two vessels to be slipped, and headed out for deeper water. The passage back to Holyhead was far from easy with gigantic seas following the lifeboat as she steamed through the darkness along the exposed north coast of Holyhead Island. Harbour was eventually reached, however, and the nine men were thankfully landed into the hands of the Sailors' Home at 7pm.

The *Harold* was wrecked the next morning between the two Stacks.

This rescue by William Owen, which gained him the RNLI gold medal for gallantry, so impressed the Prince of Wales (later King George V), who was President of the Institution at the time, that he commanded the Welsh coxswain to attend at Marlborough House where he would himself present the medal.

The ten others members of Coxswain Owen's crew each received the silver medal for their part in the rescue. The medals were presented to them at a special function at Holyhead Town Hall by the President of the lifeboat station branch, The Lord Stanley of Alderley.

A technical drawing of the Duke of Northumberland, the first steam lifeboat to be built by the RNLI in 1891, and the boat in which Holyhead coxswain, William Owen, won his gold medal seventeen years later. The boat was 50ft long, weighed 30 tons, was capable of some 9 knots and was driven, not by screws, but by a hydraulic system of propulsion with a pump which sucked water through an inlet in the bottom of the boat and expelled it under water through outlets pointing towards bow or stern, depending on the required direction of travel. (Drawing reproduced by courtesy of Shipping World and Shipbuilder.)

9

THE *ROHILLA* RESCUE

Off Whitby, 30 October 1914

Gold Medals to Coxswain Thomas Langlands, Whitby; Coxswain Robert Smith, Tynemouth;
and Captain H.E. Burton, Royal Engineers

'The services rendered in connexion with the wreck of the hospital ship *Rohilla* have added another splendid page to the annals of heroism and humanity which make up the story of the Life-boat during the ninety years since the foundation of the Institution.'

The *Lifeboat* journal, February 1915.

More than three-quarters of a century have passed since the account of the wreck of the *Rohilla* and the survivors' rescue was published in the *Lifeboat*, yet it still stands out as one of the most historic of all sea rescue stories.

No fewer than six lifeboats were involved, from stations as far apart as Tynemouth and Scarborough. The rescue took place over a period of two and a half days at the end of which three men had won the RNLI gold medal for gallantry and two more the silver medal. The event also proved a watershed in lifeboat technology as it illustrated in dramatic style the superiority of the motor-powered lifeboat over its pulling and sailing counterparts.

World War I had called into government service the steamer *Rohilla*, a 7,400-ton vessel of the British India Line. Converted into a hospital ship, she was on her way from Queensferry to Dunkirk where she would embark wounded from the line. She had 229 people on board, which included crew and medical staff. Shortly after 4am on 30 October 1914, in an east-south-easterly gale, she ran onto a reef of rocks at Saltwick Nab to the south and east of Whitby.

Immediately the ship struck she broke in half in the mountainous seas. Those unfortunate enough to be on the aft part were washed away at once and drowned.

Daybreak was the earliest the people of Whitby could begin their attempt to rescue those who had survived the initial tragedy. By an extraordinary effort the town's No 2 lifeboat *John Fielden* was manhandled to the scene of the wreck. As well as hauling her along the rocky foreshore the launchers somehow got the three-ton lifeboat over an eight-foot sea wall.

The wreck lay about a quarter of a mile from the spot where the lifeboat's coxswain, Thomas Langlands, decided to launch. He did so knowing that the lifeboat had been stove in in two places during her improbable journey to the beach.

Amid great waves the lifeboat reached the *Rohilla* and took off twelve men and five women. These survivors were unceremoniously offloaded in the surf back at the beach while the lifeboat launched again. One of the five women, all of whom were nurses, must have wondered if she was the most or least fortunate person to have lived. Her name was Mary Roberts and only three years earlier she had taken a job aboard a brand new transatlantic liner, *SS Titanic*. History does not relate whether she ever went to sea a third time.

Again the lifeboat reached the wreck after a fearful struggle and eighteen more

Fifth from the bow on the port side of the lifeboat is nurse Mary Roberts, who is giving assistance to an injured sailor. This was her first voyage after surviving the sinking of the Titanic.

Langlands surfs in with a boat full of survivors from the Rohilla *hospital ship. The* John Fielden *brought off two boat loads before being irreparably holed. The bow and stern of* Rohilla *have broken away, giving her a peculiar appearance.*

bedraggled survivors were pulled aboard. Heavy seas which swept through or broke over the wreck filled the lifeboat as she was held alongside. Miraculously, once more her crew pulled her back to the shore but by now she could not return to the wreck. The rocks around the *Rohilla* had taken their toll on the hull and the lifeboat would not have made it a third time.

The lifeboat stationed at Upgang, two miles along the coast, was now urgently called for. Another remarkable overland journey, through the town, across fields to the top of the cliffs and then by rope precipitously down to the beach was accomplished by scores of willing helpers to bring the Upgang lifeboat to the scene. The weather had the final say, however. The huge seas forced even these desperate lifeboatmen to forestall another launch to the *Rohilla*.

Telephone messages had by now reached Scarborough to the south and Teesmouth to the north. To begin with Scarborough lifeboat's attempts to leave the harbour were thwarted by the wild sea, but finally at 3.30pm she was clear, under tow from a steam trawler.

When she arrived at the scene it was dark and any rescue attempt would have been suicidal. Nevertheless, her crew remained at sea the entire night in hellish conditions hoping for a chance to do something. But by daybreak on the Saturday morning it was obvious that still nothing could be done and forlornly they returned to Scarborough.

The courageous intent of the lifeboatmen of Teesmouth was just as great. They waited until the Saturday morning before they set out, knowing that daylight was essential to their task. But in the mountainous waves they encountered as they were towed across the Tees bar the lifeboat crashed deep into a trough, sprang a serious leak and had to be evacuated by the tug towing her and returned to Middlesbrough.

TOP RIGHT: Thomas Langlands, coxswain of Whitby lifeboat, who, in the pulling lifeboat, John Fielden, *twice reached the wreck of the hospital ship* Rohilla *amid great waves and rocks, and brought thirty-five back to the beach and safety.*

RIGHT: Coxswain Robert Smith of Tynemouth, who took his new motor lifeboat, Henry Vernon, *forty-four miles in huge seas and darkness to reach Whitby. It was the motor lifeboat which was eventually able to draw alongside the* Rohilla *and take off the remaining fifty survivors from the wreck.*

Early on the Saturday morning, meanwhile, back at the beach the crew of Upgang lifeboat were prepared once again to attempt the seemingly impossible. At 9am they launched, but immediately it was clear that the sea and current were too strong. Once the lifeboat got as close as fifty yards from the wreck before her exhausted crew were forced back.

To see the lifeboat return unsuccessfully to the beach yet again was too much for some of the *Rohilla*'s survivors. To the astonishment of those on shore people could be seen leaping into the water in a desperate effort to swim to the shore. Onlookers heroically plunged into the surf to pull many of them to safety. But they could not save them all. Several were drowned.

A final attempt by Whitby lifeboatmen was made to reach the wreck when the town's No 1 lifeboat, as yet unprevailed upon, cleared the harbour under the command of Coxswain Thomas Langlands and was towed by a Hartlepool trawler to within half a mile of the *Rohilla*. But even Thomas Langlands, who had twice got alongside the previous day, had to admit defeat and return to harbour.

The position of the wreck as well as the atrocious weather were the main cause of the pulling lifeboats' difficulties. The rocks amongst which she lay provided no anchorage to allow a boat to veer down upon her. Perhaps a new motor lifeboat could drive in and out without the need for an anchor.

Tynemouth had such a boat. At 4.15 on the Saturday afternoon Tynemouth lifeboat headed into the North Sea in response to a telegrammed call for help. In command was Coxswain Robert Smith, accompanied by Captain H.E. Burton RE, an expert in the workings of the new petrol engine and the Honorary Superintendent of the motor lifeboat. At 1am on the Sunday morning the lifeboat was in Whitby harbour. She had steamed forty-four miles in huge seas, darkness and with no coast lights on account of the war; some achievement in navigation and endurance in itself.

Four hours after her arrival at Whitby the Tynemouth lifeboat set out again for the wreck, having embarked a quantity of oil for possible use to calm the sea, and a Lifeboat Inspector, Commander Basil Hall, who had been despatched from London HQ on news of the disaster.

The crew of the Whitby No 2 lifeboat, John Fielden, *photographed after the* Rohilla *rescue.*

The rest of the story is splendidly recounted by the following extracts taken from an eyewitness account which appeared in a contemporary edition of the *Yorkshire Post.*

'The light was just rising over the sea at half past six o'clock when I saw the boat creep out of the harbour again and breast the breakers like a sea bird as she headed straight out into calmer water. Hastening, with others, to the top of the cliffs south of the town, I rejoined the crowd of watchers there, who gazed with eager intensity as the lifeboat, looking fearfully small and frail, rode easily on the waves and throbbed her way towards the wreck. Nearer and nearer she got; and then, when within 200 yards of the *Rohilla,* she turned seawards.

'Was she unable to face the current running at four knots an hour and the curling seas, still fierce and strong, though of diminished size? "She'll never get there," declared one of the watchers. But a burly fisherman remarked, "Just wait; she knows what she's about." Presently, when she had passed a few fathoms beyond and away from the wreck, she stopped dead and discharged over the boiling sea gallons and gallons of oil. It seemed that the ocean must laugh at these puny drops, yet the effect was remarkable; within a few seconds, as the oil spread over the surface of the water and was carried by the current towards the wreck, the waves appeared suddenly to be flattened down as by a miracle, all round the vessel's bridge, leaving a gently undulating sea. In the meantime the lifeboat turned about, raced at full speed outside the line of breakers, past the stern of the wreck, and then turned directly to the shore. The most dangerous moment came when she was inside the surf and broadside on to the waves; but, guided with splendid skill and courage, she moved forward steadily and a cheer of relief went out from the shore when she reached the lee of the wreck, immediately beneath the crowded bridge. The feelings of those on board as they saw salvation at hand can only be imagined.

'But there was not a moment to be lost, for already the effects of the oil were beginning to pass off, and the waves were noticeably higher. Quicker than thought a rope was let down to the lifeboat, and immediately figures could be discerned scrambling down into the boat with a quickness and agility that seemed extraordinary in men one presumed to be exhausted almost to death. In less than a quarter of an hour more than forty men had been taken into the boat. It was then, while the rest were preparing to leave the wreck, that two enormous waves were seen rolling up from the sea at tremendous speed. One after the other they swept over the bridge and across each end of the remnants of the deck onto the lifeboat at the other side, enveloping it fore and aft. Each time the tough little craft disappeared for a moment beneath the spray, reappeared, tottered, and righted herself gamely. Indeed, not a man was lost, not a splinter broken. Closer still she hugged the vessel's side till every man aboard – fifty of them in all – had been hauled into the rescuing boat.

'The last man to leave his lost ship was the captain, and as he slipped into the lifeboat the crew of the latter gave a rousing cheer that was echoed again and again by the people ashore.

'But the peril was not yet over; another crisis had to be met before anxiety was allayed. As the lifeboat shot past the wreck on her return journey she was struck broadside on by a great wave that threatened to throw her on her beam ends; but once more she manfully withstood the shock, and swept gaily out to sea in a wide semi-circle that brought her safely to the harbour mouth.'

Among the many awards made following this historic incident, the RNLI's gold medal was awarded to Coxswain Thomas Langlands of Whitby, and Coxswain Robert Smith and Captain H.E. Burton of Tynemouth. Second Coxswain Richard Eglon of Whitby No 2 lifeboat and Second Coxswain James Brownlee of Tynemouth lifeboat received the Institution's silver medal, together with their Inspector, Commander Basil Hall.

Tynemouth's 40ft motor lifeboat, Henry Vernon, *back on the Tyne not long after her heroic service to the* Rohilla.

10

THE WRECK OF THE *SS FERNEBO*

Off Cromer, 9 January 1917

Coxswain Henry Blogg's first Gold Medal

Those who live by the sea will know that from time to time a wave will come that is a giant in comparison with all the others being cast upon the shore. Statistics even exist to show that one wave in 1,175 will be three times higher than the normal.

No statistics will be found to prove how frequently the sea produces a man who stands out as prominently above his fellow seamen, but one such must surely have been Henry Blogg of Cromer, Norfolk. He was coxswain of the lifeboat there from 1909 until 1948, in which time, spanning two world wars, he helped to save 873 lives and won a still unequalled record of three gold medals and four silver, all for outstanding bravery.

It is no exaggeration to say that his exploits off the coast of Norfolk did more than anything else to endear the RNLI to the British public in the first half of the twentieth century. Blogg in his day was as well known and popular a hero as any star of screen or sportsfield might be today.

The comparison is not altogether inappropriate; often it was as though he were carrying out his life-and-death struggles with the sea in a huge public arena. Whenever the lifeboat was called out, practically the whole town would turn out, to lend a hand with launching if they could or simply to watch and cheer on their coxswain and crew. In the summer their numbers were swelled even more by holiday-makers.

But on the morning of 9 January 1917, there was no holiday spirit among those on the beach. World War I had already entered its third soul-destroying year, a freezing north-easterly gale had been blowing hard at the town all night off the sea and huge breakers were crashing onto the shore.

The lifeboat was out. Henry Blogg and his ageing crew (at least two were nearly seventy) were battling through the surf towards a small Greek steamer, the *Pyrin*, which was on the verge of being driven ashore, having fought bravely all night to ride out the storm, steaming up to her anchor.

Thanks to the war, the only young men available to Cromer that day were a group of soldiers who happened to be billeted in the town. They had helped the locals to launch the 38ft Liverpool class lifeboat, *Louisa Heartwell*, a while earlier. It had been an immense struggle against the surf; the launchers had had to enter deep water, up to their waists and further, to allow the lifeboat on her carriage to

Coxswain Henry Blogg at the tiller of his lifeboat the Louisa Heartwell. *The stern half of the Swedish steamship* Fernebo *can be seen in the surf off Cromer; her crew anxiously watch as Blogg's ageing crew strain at their oars to get near.*

Blogg and his crew battle their way through the surf to reach the Swedish steamer Fernebo. *This picture shows an early attempt to clear the surf, with a large wave ahead about to hurl the boat back to the shore.*

Coxswain Henry Blogg still holds the record number of medals won. In all, he received three gold and four silver, each representing a separate feat of outstanding bravery. He is seen here being presented with his second gold medal by the RNLI President, HRH Edward, Prince of Wales, at the 1928 Annual General Meeting of the Institution following his service to the Dutch oil tanker Georgia *in November 1927.*

Three to four miles out the Swedish steamship *Fernebo* had lost control with engine trouble and had drifted onto a mine. The explosion amidships split her clean in half and from the beach the onlookers gazed in amazement as they could see, through a billow of smoke and steam, two halves of a ship drifting slowly apart from each other.

What was so strange was that both halves remained upright and fully afloat. The explanation, they later learned, was that the ship had been loaded high with timber, making her exceptionally stable and buoyant. Partly because of this and partly by extreme good fortune, only one man, the chief engineer, had so far been lost as the ship broke in two.

Surely the Cromer lifeboat crew could not be expected to put out again? Were not the neighbouring crews at Palling and Sheringham fresh and able to go? Messages very soon came back that the state of the sea made it impossible for either boat to launch. Either the Cromer boat went or the men on the Swedish steamer perished.

There was no real choice for Blogg and his men in spite of their aching limbs. Like battered and over-age prize fighters climbing back into the ring for a second bout, they once more took up their positions in the lifeboat. The tide was higher now and the waves were even more mountainous.

negotiate a low bank of sand before she could be released into the sea. Twice the lifeboat and carriage had been hurled back towards the beach by the strength of the waves but finally she was away.

The sodden launchers now watched anxiously as the lifeboat was swept off course, a mile to the westward, narrowly missing the end of the pier while her crew pulled with all their might on the oars to bring her clear of danger.

Once she was able to set sail the task became more straightforward, but already Blogg and his men had been at sea for over two hours and by the time the lifeboat had run alongside the steamer, pulled her crew of sixteen aboard and returned to the beach, another hour of full exertion by her crew had elapsed. The men were utterly exhausted.

As if the force 9 gale was not enough for shipping in that area to contend with that day, another deadly danger lurked just off the coast. At 3pm, while the *Pyrin*'s crew were still being disembarked from the lifeboat, a great explosion could be heard out to sea.

Willing launchers hauled the lifeboat to the edge of the surf and after a struggle they got her afloat. For half an hour her crew pulled with all their remaining strength to try to clear the surf, but it was in vain. The lifeboat was beaten back to the shore.

Meanwhile, aboard the remains of the *Fernebo* a desperate attempt was being made by six of her crew to save themselves. A small boat had been launched into the waves and in defiance of what appeared to be imminent capsize, was gradually approaching the beach. Fifty yards from the shore the boat was hurled upside down in the surf.

Led by Private Stewart Holmes of the 2nd/4th Seaforth Highlanders, rescuers from the shore rushed into the waves, linking hands in a human chain, to pull the half-drowned seamen from the water. Miraculously, all six were saved. Private Holmes, who himself was all but drowned, would later receive the RNLI silver medal for his courage. Another soldier, Private Sharpe, of the Army Service Corps, never recovered from the exposure he received that day and developed permanent paralysis.

At about 5pm, two hours after the explosion, the two halves of the *Fernebo* ran aground close to the shore, the foremost end about half a mile further east than the after end where all the survivors were.

Immediately line-throwing guns were brought forward, as well as some powerful searchlights lent by the army which clearly illuminated the frantic crewmen on the aft part of the wreck. The stage was lit for the final act of this grim drama. The crowd stood and watched as rocket line after rocket line was fired towards the broken ship. She was barely four hundred feet away abreast of a long wooden groyne and yet the ferocious wind made a mockery of these attempts at accuracy. Every line missed by a wide margin.

Enter Coxswain Blogg. He and his men had had four hours' respite and they were now prepared to try again to reach the wreck. Commander Basil Hall, the Inspector of Lifeboats (who just over two years earlier had been actively involved in the famous *Rohilla* rescue at Whitby, and who was now on the beach at Cromer directing the proceedings), was reluctant to let the lifeboat go. He knew how tired the crew still were. He did not stand in their way, however. His own eyewitness account of the events takes up the story.

'For half an hour these splendid men made the most gallant attempt to reach the vessel – over and over again the boat was swept back into the shallow water inshore, but each time they succeeded in keeping her head on to the sea and pulling her out again into the deeper water about halfway between the ship and the shore.

'Bathed in the brilliant beam of the searchlight, one moment standing on end as she mounted the crest of a huge breaker, at another with her nose buried in the trough of the sea, or completely lost to sight as a sea broke right over her, the lifeboat made a sight which will never be forgotten by the hundreds of spell-bound spectators who lined the beach.

'I myself would not have believed it possible for even a strong and young crew to do so much with this heavy boat. It was not till five oars had been broken and three more washed ashore, whilst the boat was approaching dangerously the end of the groyne, that the coxswain gave up and allowed his boat to come to the shore.'

Henry Blogg's exploits off the coast of Norfolk probably did more than anything else to endear the RNLI to the British public in the first half of the twentieth century.

Yet more unsuccessful attempts were made to fire lines from the shore to the ship. Then to everyone's consternation Henry Blogg announced to his head launcher, Tom Bussey, that he was going to have another go.

He had seen a chance of launching the lifeboat at a point on the beach where the tide had begun to create a current which swept almost out to the wreck. A fourth agonising launching sequence ensued, followed by more breathtaking moments as the lifeboat crept closer and closer to her destination.

At last she was alongside and men were seen being pulled aboard the lifeboat. After what seemed an age to the onlookers, Coxswain Blogg headed the lifeboat back towards the beach and, to spontaneous cheering from the crowd, the ship's remaining complement of eleven men were helped out of the lifeboat once she was safely ashore. The time was 1am.

This was the first gold medal Henry Blogg was to be awarded in his unequalled career. His acting second coxswain, William Davies, received the silver medal and the rest of the lifeboat crew became the first to be awarded the newly instituted bronze medal for gallantry.

11

THE DAUNT ROCK LIGHTSHIP RESCUE

Off Ballycotton, 13 February 1936

Gold Medal to Coxswain Patrick Sliney, Ballycotton

A theme common to many of the stories behind the award of the RNLI gold medal is the element of human endurance. The length of time rescuers have tolerated the extreme conditions and traumas leading up to the moment of actual life-saving is often remarkable. When Coxswain Patrick Sliney and his Ballycotton crewmen finally returned to station on 14 February 1936 after rescuing the crew of the Daunt Rock lightship, the lifeboat had been away for over three days, forty-nine hours of which had been spent at sea in hurricane-force winds.

It is the custom of the RNLI that an account of every service carried out by a lifeboat is submitted to headquarters by the station honorary secretary. There can have been few more vivid or moving descriptions received than that of Ballycotton honorary secretary Robert H. Mahony following this historic rescue. His story begins:

'On Friday, 7th February, 1936, a gale from the south-east sprang up on the south coast of Ireland, with a very heavy sea. The gale increased until, about midnight on Monday, 10th it was blowing a hurricane force never before experienced by the oldest inhabitant in Ballycotton. Huge waves were smashing over the pier and breakwater. The harbour was a seething cauldron. At high water on the Monday evening, nothing could be seen of the breakwater or the pier.

'During the Sunday and early on Monday the coxswain ran ropes from the lifeboat, the *Mary Stanford*, a 51 feet Barnett cabin motor lifeboat, to prevent her from striking the breakwater. At midnight on the Monday, when the gale had risen to a hurricane, the coxswain's own motor boat was seen to have parted her moorings, and was in danger of being carried out to sea. The coxswain and several other men attempted to launch a boat to her, but were nearly swamped. Stones, a ton in weight, were being torn from the quay and flung about like sugar lumps. I spent most of the night near the lifeboat house, watching the terrible destruction that the wind and waves were doing. Twice I was spun round and nearly flung on my face. At three on the Tuesday morning I went to bed, but not to sleep. I was out again shortly after seven, and found that the coxswain and the other men had been up all night trying to secure his motor boat. They had succeeded in launching a boat, got a rope to the motor boat and secured her. It was at that moment, after this long night of anxiety, that the call for the lifeboat came.

'The men were just back, at eight o'clock, when the Civic Guard at Ballycotton rang me up. A messenger had arrived (all telephone communication except by the land lines had broken down twenty-four hours before) with a message that the Daunt Rock Lightship, with eight men on board, had broken from her moorings twelve miles away, and was drifting towards Ballycotton.

Happy family ending: Coxswain Patrick Sliney (left), his wife and crewmember son William pictured outside the RNLI headquarters in Grosvenor Gardens, London, before the two men from Ballycotton, Co. Cork received their medals for bravery following the Daunt Rock lightship rescue of 1936. Patrick was awarded the gold medal and William the bronze.

The lifeboat hails the Daunt Rock lightship to discover her intentions. The ship's crew would not leave their vessel as they knew the danger to shipping an abandoned lightship would present.

55

'I gave the coxswain the message and he made no reply. I had seen the weather. Seas were breaking over the lifeboat house, where the boarding boat was kept. I did not believe it was possible for the coxswain even to get aboard the lifeboat at her moorings. I was afraid to order him out.

'He left and went down to the harbour. I followed a little later. To my amazement the lifeboat was already at the harbour mouth, dashing out between the piers. The coxswain had not waited for orders. His crew were already at the harbour. He had not fired the maroons, for he did not want to alarm the village. Without a word they had slipped away. As I watched the lifeboat I thought every minute she must turn back. At one moment a sea crashed on her; at the next she was standing on her heel. But she went on. People watching her left the quay to go to the church to pray. I watched till she was a mile off, at the lighthouse, where she met seas so mountainous that their spray, as we could see (and the lighthouse keeper verified it), was flying over the lantern 196 feet high. At the lighthouse the lifeboat seemed to hesitate. She turned round. We thought she was coming back. Then to our horror the coxswain took her through the sound between the two islands. That way, as we knew, though it was much more dangerous than the open sea, he would save half a mile.

'He took her through the sound, after consulting with his second coxswain, and there, so he told me afterwards, the seas were tremendous. The lifeboat came off the top of one sea and dropped into the trough of the next with such a terrible thud that everyone thought the engines had gone through the bottom of the boat, but the motor mechanic reported: "All's well. After that she will go through anything." The coxswain had the whole crew in the after cockpit. After each sea had filled it he counted his men.'

Safely through the sound and now about six miles from Ballycotton, Coxswain Sliney found the following seas were worse still. During the process of putting out a drogue, waves continually swept over the lifeboat, half-stunning the coxswain as they crashed over his head. The largest wave filled the cockpit and knocked every crewman off his feet.

Visibility was appalling in the spray and sleet. The lightship could not be found and finally the coxswain decided to run for Queenstown for information.

The pilots at Queenstown were able to give an exact position; the lifeboat set out again and soon after midday found the lightship a quarter of a mile south-west of the Daunt Rock and only half a mile from the shore. Her crew would not leave her, knowing the danger an abandoned lightvessel out of position would present to shipping. They feared their anchor would not hold, however, and asked the lifeboat to stand by.

Also standing by was the Royal Navy destroyer, *HMS Tenedos*, and from about 3.30pm, when the gale had eased a little, until darkness two hours later, attempts were made to establish a tow between the lightship and the destroyer. Even when the lifeboat was twice able to pass the line aboard the casualty, the line parted. All the time the three vessels were being swept by heavy seas.

Towing attempts became impossible once darkness had fallen and, with *HMS Tenedos* prepared to stand by all night, Coxswain Sliney decided to make for Queenstown. He needed more rope and, more importantly, his wet and exhausted crew needed food. Harbour was reached at 9.30pm.

The drawn faces of men recently returned from a rescue which took more than three days to complete in hurricane force winds. The crew of Ballycotton lifeboat saved eight men from the Daunt Rock lightvessel in their ordeal.

Robert Mahony, the honorary secretary, had been spending the time his lifeboat was away desperately trying to keep track of her progress. Fallen trees across roads and telephone lines down made his task virtually impossible. Finally, at 11pm on the Tuesday night he made contact with Queenstown by telephone:

'I spoke to the coxswain. He told me the position, and I went back at once to Ballycotton and set out for Queenstown with a spare drogue, tripping line and veering lines, and changes of underclothing for the crew. It was twenty-three miles to Queenstown, and again a very difficult journey by night, dodging fallen trees. I arrived at Queenstown at three in the morning of Wednesday 12th, handed over the stores and returned to Ballycotton.

'Some of the crew had managed to get a little sleep, but there were three of the crew in the lifeboat all the time, ready if a call came. Early in the morning of the 12th the lifeboat set out again. *HMS Tenedos* left, but the *Isolda*, the vessel of the Irish Lights, was expected from Dublin. The wind dropped a little during this, the second day. Fog set in. But the sea did not seem to go down. The lifeboat stood by all day. When the wireless weather report was received at six in the evening the lightship again asked the lifeboat to continue standing by. She stood by all night.

'At daylight on the 13th, which was shortly after seven, the coxswain decided to make again for Queenstown as his petrol was getting low. She reached Queenstown at nine on the morning of the 13th. She had then been standing by for twenty-five and a half hours. The seas had been breaking continually over her crew, and they had had no food.

'I had 160 gallons of petrol ready at Ballycotton but it was impossible to get a motor lorry. I telephoned to Cork to send her eighty gallons but the driver of the lorry injured his arm. A second driver had to be got. There was a delay. As soon as the lifeboat had the petrol she set out again. It was then four in the afternoon.

'When the lifeboat reached the lightvessel again, about dusk, she found that the *Isolda* had arrived. Her captain told the coxswain that he intended to stand by all night and in the morning would try to take the lightship in tow. But the weather since four o'clock had been getting worse. At eight o'clock a big sea went over the lightship, carrying away the forward of the two red lights which are hoisted by a lightship at bow and stern to show that she is out of position. At 9.30, with the wind and sea still increasing, the coxswain took the lifeboat round the lightship's stern, with his searchlight playing on her. In its light he could see her crew, with their lifebelts on, and the seas breaking over them, huddled at the stern. The wind, which had been south-east, had gone to south-south-east. The lightship was now, the coxswain estimated, not more than sixty yards from the Daunt Rock. He went to the *Isolda* and told her captain that the lightship was now in great danger. She was very near the rock. She was to the south-west of it. The wind was shifting. If it went a bit to the west, she must strike the rock.

'The captain said that in the heavy sea it was impossible for the *Isolda* to do anything. The coxswain asked if he should try to take the crew off. He was told to carry on. He took the lifeboat round the lightship again. The seas were going right over her. She was plunging tremendously on her cable, rolling from 30 to 40 degrees, burying her starboard bow in the water and throwing her stern all over the place. She was fitted with rolling chocks, which projected over two feet from her sides, and as she rolled these threshed the water.

'To anchor to windward and drop down to her was impossible, owing to her cable. The only thing was to get astern and make quick runs in on her port side, calling on her crew to jump for the lifeboat as they could. The coxswain went within hailing distance and told the lightship's crew what he intended to do. He must run in at full speed, check for a second, then go full speed astern. In that second, the men must jump. He knew the dangers. The lightship was only 98 feet long. If he ran too far, the lifeboat would go over her cable and be capsized. As he came alongside, the lightship, with her chocks threshing the water as she plunged and rolled, might crash over right on top of the lifeboat.

'The coxswain went ahead of the lightship, pumped out oil to calm the seas a little (but the tide was running strongly and the effect of the oil did not last long), went astern of her and then drove full speed alongside. One man jumped, and the lifeboat went astern. A second time she raced in, but no one jumped; a third time, and five men jumped; a fourth time – the lightship sheered violently and her counter crashed on top of the lifeboat, smashing the rails and damaging the fender and deck. No one was hurt, but the man working the searchlight sprang clear only just in time. The lifeboat went in a fifth time. Again no one jumped.

'There were still two men on board the lightvessel. They were clinging to the rails. They seemed unable to jump. The coxswain sent some of his crew forward, at the risk of being swept overboard, with orders to seize the two men as the lifeboat came

alongside. Then he raced in for the sixth time. The men were seized and dragged in. As the coxswain said, it was no time for "By your leave." One of the men had his face knocked against either the fluke of the anchor or the stanchion and badly cut. The other man's legs were hurt. The motor mechanic was able, with iodine and bandages, to give first aid to the man whose face was cut. Shortly after the rescue one of the men of the lightvessel (the long strain on them had been tremendous) became hysterical, and two men had to hold him down to prevent anyone from being hurt or knocked overboard.

'The lifeboat, after reporting to *Isolda*, made for Queenstown, where she arrived at eleven on the night of 13th February, and the two injured men were taken to hospital. The lifeboat remained at Queenstown for the night, returning next morning to Ballycotton where she arrived at 12.45pm.'

Sliney hails the Daunt Rock lightship with a speaking trumpet.

12

RESCUE
FROM THE TRAWLER *GURTH*

Near the Humber mouth, 12 February 1940

Gold Medal to Coxswain Robert Cross, Humber

Crewing the lifeboat during either of the two world wars, something which through necessity often fell to the older men of the community, was an even more dangerous occupation than in peacetime. It was not only the elements that crews had to contend with but hazards such as blacked-out harbours, mines, and possible enemy air attacks as well.

When, on the night of 12 February 1940, a freezing north-easterly gale sprang up with snow and a four-knot tide running out of the Humber, every element of both war and nature combined to make it a time to stay by the hearth if humanly possible.

But, war or no war, fishermen had still to earn their keep and the trawler *Gurth* was returning that night to Grimsby when the onshore gale caught her. She was swept past the entrance to the Humber estuary and was in imminent danger of driving ashore just to the south.

The lifeboat station at Spurn Head, a narrow spit of land protruding into the estuary, was short-handed when the distress call came. Normally eight men would take the lifeboat out, but only seven were living in that remote spot at the time. Worse still, two of them were ill. One, the assistant mechanic, Samuel Cross (no relation to the coxswain), immediately left his sick-bed when the assembly bell rang and asked the coxswain to take him, knowing six men, at the very least, would be needed on a night like that.

Coxswain Robert Cross steered the 35ft 6in Watson class lifeboat, *City of Bradford II*, out of the comparative shelter of the estuary, and as the full force of the gale struck, he caught sight of a light which appeared to be moving swiftly towards the shore. The light was indeed coming from the *Gurth* but before the lifeboat could reach her she had struck. Immediately the surf swept over her so that only her forecastle remained above water, providing the only refuge for her nine-man crew.

Coxswain Cross had a nearly impossible task on his hands. Both conventional means of approaching a vessel aground in the surf were ruled out. He could not veer down on his anchor stern-first towards the trawler because the fierce tide, running at right-angles to his approach, would carry him far off course. The tide also prevented him running alongside the lee side of the trawler (not that much lee existed), because its strength would surely wash him right on top of her.

To the men on the trawler, if they could see anything of the lifeboat's manoeuvres from their precarious position, the coxswain's chosen course of action must at first have appeared a failure. He had anchored 160 yards to seaward of them and was veering down towards the shore, huge seas bearing down on his bow as he went. Further and further the lifeboat crept until she was lying almost parallel with the grounded trawler. The tide, however, had carried the lifeboat 150 yards away from her down the coast.

But Robert Cross was a hugely resourceful seaman. Every move he made had been planned. Ten yards from the shore he had sent the assistant mechanic forward to fasten a rope to the anchor cable. The man was then to bring the end back again to one of the bollards astern. Now the lifeboat paid out ten more yards of anchor cable until she was actually in the breaking surf.

The six lifeboatmen from Spurn Point who saved nine from the stranded trawler Gurth *at the mouth of the Humber in February 1940. They are (l to r) Sam Hoopell, Assistant Mechanic Samuel Cross, Coxswain Robert Cross, Second Coxswain W.R. Jenkinson, Bowman William Hood and Motor Mechanic John Major. (Photograph by kind permission of Vera Cross, daughter of Coxswain Robert Cross.)*

58

Resourceful Coxswain Cross has rigged his line from the stern bollard to the anchor cable, thus enabling him to work 'uptide' to the Gurth. *This cable can be seen above the sternmost lifeboatman.*

The coxswain's next order was for the assistant mechanic to haul on his rope. Slowly the lifeboat began to swing round until her bow pointed up the coast towards the trawler. At this moment the rope was made fast.

The lifeboat crew now depended for their lives on the rope and anchor cable. If either gave way the lifeboat, broadside to the seas, would be bowled over and swept straight ashore. As it was, the bridle which held her kept her stiff against the seas and withstood their full shock. As the men took up their positions on deck, ready to receive survivors, they found themselves constantly washed off their feet by the six-foot breakers. The mechanic at the engine controls under the canopy was up to his chin in water and had to find the levers by touch in the flooded cockpit.

Meanwhile, the coxswain, without his full crew, had no one to operate the searchlight and had to make his approach practically blind. The lifeboat began to claw her painful way up towards the trawler against the tide, the bridle keeping her in her unnatural attitude, broadside to the weather.

Each man aboard the trawler had to be rescued in a single, co-ordinated movement by lifeboat and crew working with perfect timing. The lifeboat would drive in to the trawler's forecastle until the two vessels touched. At that moment the two men in the bow had to snatch one of the survivors before the coxswain put the engines astern to avoid being hurled against the casualty by the next sea.

Each time Cross worked his lifeboat City of Bradford II *up to the bows of the* Gurth, *the bowmen would grab a trawlerman and lead him below. After more than twenty approaches the whole crew were saved and landed in Grimsby.*

A photograph taken just before the outbreak of World War II, showing Spurn Point much as it would have appeared at the time of Robert Cross's gold medal rescue in 1940. The coxswain and crew lived in the houses on the right and the lifeboat station and slipway can be seen further in the distance. (Photograph by courtesy of The Topical Press Agency Ltd.)

To make the whole manoeuvre more complex still, the sick assistant mechanic, manning the rope which formed the bridle astern, was also needed in the bow to help catch the survivors at the critical moment. So, just before he scrambled forward each time, he put another turn round the bollard and left the end to be held under the coxswain's foot. Every time after the lifeboat came astern, the rope needed paying out so that the lifeboat could lie more easy for a moment head to seas, to allow the water to empty out of her. Coxswain Cross, his hands on the helm, had often to perform this task himself with his feet on the occasions his assistant mechanic could not return aft in time to pick up the rope.

Twenty approaches had achieved the rescue of six of the trawlermen. Then an engine stopped. A small rope which had been washed overboard had found its way round the propeller. In their situation there was no chance for the crew to cut it away. The coxswain was forced to continue working on only one engine. With only half the power, the dangers were far more than doubled. But the strength and skill of the coxswain and crew saw them through. Again and again they ran up to the trawler and at last the remaining three men were aboard.

Now the rope which held her stern was let go for the last time. But as the lifeboat swung round to face the seas, the stern struck the bottom. The single

engine battled to bring her clear but not before she struck several more times, splitting the rudder. Mercifully it could still steer the lifeboat out to her anchor. At this point the crew, having brought the anchor up, were able to open the scuttle over the fouled propeller and cut away the rope.

It was 8am when the Humber lifeboat approached Grimsby harbour. She had been at sea eleven hours. The coxswain had asked special permission to have the harbour lights switched on for his return but even at that hour it was still so dark and the snow so thick that the lifeboat's searchlight was needed to find the harbour entrance.

Those who saw the disembarkation said that the lifeboat crew appeared even more exhausted than the survivors. The lifeboat herself bore several reminders of the ordeal. Her skin was pierced, her bow-pudding fender torn away and most of her iron stanchions had been beaten level with the deck by the force of the seas.

The RNLI gold medal for gallantry was awarded to the sixty-four-year-old Coxswain Robert Cross and the rest of his crew received the silver medal.

Only three years later Robert Cross was to become one of the select band to receive a second gold medal. He won it rescuing nineteen men from another grounded trawler, the *Almondine*, in foul weather on 7 January 1943.

THE *SS BROWNING*
Aground at Ballyquintin, Co Down, 21 January 1942

Coxswain Patrick Murphy of Newcastle was the eventual gold medal winner for this rescue; he was called out in the motor lifeboat *L.P. and St Helen* to the assistance of seven ships from a wartime convoy which were ashore near Ballyquintin, Co Down. They had missed their way in a south-easterly gale, very heavy seas and sleet.

However, having steamed twenty miles through the worst of the gale to get there, the Newcastle lifeboat could only hope to get close to one of the ships, the *SS Browning*. Seventeen of the steamship's crew had already succeeded in reaching the shore, thanks to a life-saving apparatus, but thirty-nine were still aboard, one of whom had been shot in the hand while destroying horses. Approaches by the lifeboat from the windward side proving impossible, the coxswain was forced to the leeward, and at great danger to himself and his crew steered through a narrow channel into a lagoon of calm water alongside the wreck.

All survivors were helped aboard, although this seriously overloaded the lifeboat. However, it did not deter the coxswain from taking the only way out: judging his moment to perfection, he put the lifeboat at full speed across the reef of rocks and escaped into deep water. The survivors were landed at the fishing village of Portavogie.

With three tons of living men aboard, Pat Murphy helms the L.P. and St Helen *lifeboat over a reef on the back of a wave, thus saving all. In the background the* SS Bronxville *(from the same convoy) lies stranded.*

RESCUE FROM THE *RUNSWICK*
Peterhead, Aberdeenshire, 23–26 January 1942

Early in the morning of Friday 23 January two Whitby steamers, the *Runswick* and the *Saltwick*, collided off the Aberdeenshire coast in strong winds; under the guidance of Peterhead lifeboat, *Julia Park Barry of Glasgow*, they made hastily for the shelter of Peterhead Bay. A third refugee from the rapidly worsening weather, the *SS Fidra* of Glasgow, was soon to join the two damaged ships at their anchorage.

Twelve hours later news reached the lifeboat station that the *Runswick* had been driven onto the rocks by the now gale-force winds. In spite of darkness, a blinding snowstorm and high seas, Coxswain John McLean located the stricken ship and brought the lifeboat close enough for lines to be secured between the two vessels. The steamer's entire crew of 44 were thus taken off.

In the next twenty-four hours the storm grew to a hurricane, with 105mph gusts blowing right into the bay. It meant the end for the other two ships at anchor; by 4pm on the Sunday both were aground. At 2am on the Monday the lifeboat was back at sea, attending the most urgent case, the *Fidra*, which was about to break up in the mountainous seas. She lay head on to the weather, providing no lee for the lifeboat. Coxswain McLean risked all as he turned head to sea and ran alongside the casualty. Only because of his extraordinary seamanship was he able to keep the boat there for 50 minutes while 26 men chose their moment to leap to safety. They were scarcely ashore when the plight of the men on the *Saltwick* became desperate. Their ship was now lying over on her starboard side on the beach with seas breaking right over her. This time his only approach to the casualty was between her and the shore. First a wave deposited the lifeboat upon some rocks, then another nearly washed every lifeboatman overboard. But he made it to the sheltered side of the wreck in spite of a severely damaged boat, and 36 survivors were helped on board. Coxswain McLean was rightly awarded the gold medal for these rescues.

The Peterhead lifeboat powers her way through heavy seas to the assistance of the Runswick, Saltwick *and* Fidra.

13

THE CANADIAN FRIGATE
CHEBOGUE AGROUND

Port Talbot Bar, 11 October 1944

Gold Medal to Coxswain William Gammon, The Mumbles

Early in October 1944 the Canadian frigate *HMCS Chebogue* is in mid-Atlantic. It is the fifth night of her westbound crossing, escorting convoy *ONS 33*, when contact is made with an enemy German submarine.

Chebogue is detached to attack the raider but, with a full moon rising astern of her, she presents an easy target for her intended quarry. A torpedo from the U-boat strikes her stern causing heavy damage and numerous casualties. The blow is not fatal, however, and she does not sink.

Injured and excess crew are taken off and the crippled warship is towed by a series of different craft the 890 miles back to British waters. The last to take her in tow is the ocean tug *Earner* which arrives in Swansea Bay with her charge soon after midday on 11 October.

The weather suddenly deteriorates. It takes only three hours for the wind from the west to reach force 9, gusting to hurricane force, and for a steep, heavy sea to develop. The *Earner* keeps her engines running in an attempt to keep the frigate's head to wind but when the tow parts, the tug, now damaged herself, is forced to make for deeper water. The frigate drifts helplessly across the bay until her stern grounds heavily on Port Talbot bar.

All telephone lines have been brought down by the gale but eventually the word gets through to The Mumbles coxswain, William Gammon, that he is urgently required. The crew is summoned. Wartime has deprived the village of its young men. No one under forty is available and two of the eight-man crew are in their seventies.

When they hear where the frigate has fetched up there is a moment's silence among them. Forty-one years earlier The Mumbles lifeboat capsized on Port Talbot bar and six of her crew were drowned. One of the survivors from that disaster is on the crew today.

But they have great faith in their present lifeboat, the motor-driven Watson class *Edward Prince of Wales*. At 7.15pm she launches into the darkness and the gale. The lifeboat flies before the wind towards the bar where the warship lies but with seas crashing over her and in the hail squalls and pitch darkness, Coxswain Gammon can scarcely make her out.

Coxswain Willam Gammon of The Mumbles; less than three years after his gold medal service to the Chebogue, *he was to lose his life with the rest of the crew when the lifeboat overturned going to the aid of the steamer,* Samtampa. *(Photograph by courtesy of Jack Thomas).*

William Gammon helms the Edward Prince of Wales *expertly over the shore break on Port Talbot Bar, having saved 42 officers and crew from the* Chebogue. *The plunging bow and anchor chains of the frigate were the most hazardous obstacle to his escape.*

He approaches within hailing distance and ascertains from the ship's commander, Lt Cdr M.F. Oliver RCNR, that he wants all his crew taken off. He cannot veer down on his anchor towards the ship for fear of fouling her anchor cable. Neither can he keep station long enough in those seas to rig a breeches buoy between the two vessels. The only possible way to get close is to head shorewards into the lethal surf, steer round the grounded stern and turn into the storm and back out to sea, pausing for a few seconds alongside the casualty on the way.

The coxswain has forty-two men to get off the frigate using this method. They are clustered on the heaving forecastle waiting for their turn to jump. Timing is all. One second the lifeboat is level with them on the deck, the next she has plunged ten, twenty feet out of sight below them. Then she has pulled away, avoiding a blow from the ship's bow as it yaws to the irregular rhythm of the gigantic seas.

Detail of the Edward Prince of Wales *crew and rescued seamen.*

Three or four men come off each time the lifeboat passes. Most manage to time their jump. Three do not. One plummets through the darkness and falls directly onto the coxswain, bruising him badly against the wheel. Another breaks his leg on landing and a third, a Lt Cdr Ian McPhee, falls into the sea between lifeboat and ship. The coxswain leaves the helm for a moment and pulls him from the water.

Twelve perilous circuits the lifeboat makes around the *Chebogue* to complete the successful evacuation of her crew. With all forty-two crowded on board, the *Edward Prince of Wales*, weighed down with her human cargo, heads into the gale back to The Mumbles where the Canadian sailors are put thankfully ashore.

William John Gammon received the gold medal for this outstanding rescue; his mechanic, William Davies, and his bowman, Thomas Ace, were awarded the bronze.

Tragically, less than three years later, on 23 August 1947, William Gammon and William Davies were both aboard the *Edward Prince of Wales* when she overturned with the loss of all hands, going to the aid of the steamer *Samtampa*.

14

THE YACHT *MAURICE GEORGES*

Saved from the rocks near St Helier, 13 September 1949

Gold Medal to Coxswain Thomas King, St Helier

Both Channel Island lifeboats, one from Jersey and one from Guernsey, were out on the afternoon of 13 September 1949. They were searching in poor weather for a French military aeroplane which had reportedly ditched in the sea somewhere to the south-east of St Helier, Jersey.

The suspicion of the crew of St Helier lifeboat that they were looking for a non-existent needle in a haystack did not deter them from carrying out a comprehensive search lasting six hours in an area stretching twenty miles from their station. All the time the sea had been rough with a fresh westerly wind and heavy rain squalls. They even encountered fog which reduced visibility to 400 yards.

Soon after 9.30pm Coxswain Thomas King, in command of the reserve Watson class lifeboat *Hearts of Oak*, temporarily on station at St Helier, was forced to head for home. His fuel was getting low. It had been a dispiriting and exhausting time at sea with the crew struggling to keep their footing on a heaving deck for hours on end as they scoured the sea through rain and fog. It was only later that they heard that the aircraft had in fact sunk on impact with the sea, taking six of her crew to the bottom, the remaining three getting themselves ashore on the French island of Chausey.

Midnight had come by the time the lifeboat drew level with the Demie de Pas beacon and her crew knew that only two more miles separated them from home port and the blissful prospect of bed.

Then a message came over the wireless. Someone had seen a light near the beacon they had just passed. Without any hesitation the coxswain swung the helm hard over and the lifeboat began to retrace her steps to investigate the light.

Four St Helier yachtsmen were at this very moment beginning to give up hope for their lives. Their 10-ton cutter, *Maurice Georges*, had left St Malo for St Helier that day on her auxiliary engine. By dusk they had reached the Demie de Pas beacon and it was there that the engine failed. The crew had no choice but to anchor on a lee shore.

The cable, however, was no match for the heavy seas and it soon parted. Before the crew had time to let go a second anchor, the yacht had been swept right among the rocks which lie to the south-east of St Helier harbour. Although the second anchor seemed to be holding, her crew knew that before long it would have to give and then nothing could prevent them being dashed onto the rocks.

Back aboard the lifeboat a terrible realisation gripped the crew when through the murky darkness they caught sight of the light from the yacht. Each man knew that if they had any chance of saving her occupants they would have to take the lifeboat in pitch darkness into an area where rocks littered the sea. The

Coxswain Thomas King of St Helier, Jersey, who took a huge risk when he steered his lifeboat among rocks in pitch darkness, an ebbing tide and heavy seas to pull a yacht to safety.

tide was ebbing, uncovering more rocks all the time, and the strong west wind blowing against the tide was making the sea very rough. As waves swept over the rocks they would disappear, then bare their angry teeth again, threatening the lifeboat as she moved in.

Coxswain King was used to a lifeboat with twin engines but the relief *Hearts of Oak* was a single-screw boat, even more vulnerable in this situation. His only reassurance was the strong build of the lifeboat for he knew that he was more likely to hit a rock than not on this mission. Men were positioned in the bow and the searchlight beam directed ahead to give some warning of rocks in the lifeboat's path.

As they came up close to the lights of the yacht, so far miraculously without mishap, a very large sea took hold of the lifeboat and washed her clean over a ledge of rock.

'That's one of the b——s passed anyhow,' remarked one of the crew.

The lifeboat was now near enough for a line to be thrown to the yachtsmen who seized it eagerly. This enabled a tow-line to be passed and made fast aboard the yacht. Her crew then cut the anchor cable and the tow back to the open sea began. Again the coxswain could only pray that he would hit nothing and of course this time he had the yacht to worry about as well.

Both vessels escaped. The entire rescue had taken only fifteen minutes but every man aboard the lifeboat knew that they had, for every second of that time, been on the edge of destruction. If ever there had been a risk taken beyond the call of duty by a lifeboat coxswain, this was one. But four yachtsmen would have died without that risk being taken.

The RNLI gold medal was presented to Thomas King following this rescue and the bronze medal went to each of the seven members of his crew. When the Inspector of Lifeboats for the area was investigating the incident for his report, he went in the lifeboat to the scene of the wreck. It was a flat calm day with clear visibility and he asked the coxswain to take the lifeboat in to the spot where the yacht was found. The coxswain refused. 'I wouldn't like to go in there now,' he said, 'we might hit something.'

Scanning the shallow water with a searchlight beam, a crew-member of Jersey's relief lifeboat Hearts of Oak *keeps a keen look-out for rocks. Another is about to throw a line to the yacht which is entrapped amongst treacherous reefs near the Demie de Pas.*

Miraculously lifted over reefs of jagged rocks by the swell, the Hearts of Oak *lifeboat arrives to assist the* Maurice Georges.
Tom King not only rescues the crew but also their boat, bringing all to safety at St Helier, with the lifeboat fuel gauges reading empty.

69

15

THE WRECK OF THE *HINDLEA*

Moelfre, Anglesey, 27 October 1959

Gold Medal to Coxswain Richard Evans, Moelfre

The scars left by the wreck of the *Royal Charter* close to the Anglesey village of Moelfre on 25 October 1859 run deep among the locals. The storm and the appalling loss of life have become a grim legend, and on the centenary of the shipwreck in October 1959 a service of remembrance was held in Llanalgo Church (where the bodies of those recovered from the wreck are buried), as it had been every year since the tragedy.

Little did Coxswain Dick Evans know, attending the centenary service with his crew, that two days later he would be battling in weather as fierce as the *Royal Charter* storm and winning in those Moelfre waters another gold medal to match that won by Joseph Rodgers a hundred years earlier.

The *Hindlea* was a coaster of 506 tons, registered in Cardiff. She had been on passage between Manchester and Newport, in ballast, when, caught by a strong south-westerly gale, she anchored in the shelter of Dulas Bay on the east coast of Anglesey. Later on that same morning of 27 October, the wind suddenly veered to the north and began to increase in strength until it had reached hurricane force with gusts up to 104mph.

From a safe haven the bay was all at once transformed into a death trap. Exposed to the full force of the wind the small coaster began to drag her anchor, and in the monstrous waves which were building up she was moving remorselessly towards the rocky shore.

On hearing that the Moelfre lifeboat was needed and why, Coxswain Dick Evans wasted no time. He knew the *Hindlea* would not have long. Dodging tiles wrenched from cottage roofs and other debris hurled about the village by the storm, he hurried to the boat-house. Only four other men had so far arrived and one, Hugh Jones, was a helper who had never been to sea in the lifeboat.

The lifeboat herself was not the usual station boat. She was the reserve 41ft Watson class lifeboat, *Edmund and Mary Robinson*, arrived only the day before to stand in while the station boat was away for refit. But even with an unfamiliar boat, only three crewmen and a shore helper (who volunteered without hesitation), Coxswain Evans launched the boat. He could not afford to wait any longer for others to arrive.

As soon as the lifeboat hit the water and turned north towards the casualty she encountered massive seas which measured twenty-five feet from trough to crest. Flying foam and scud from the broken water seriously limited the visibility. After half an hour, however, the lifeboat had fought her way to within sight of the *Hindlea*, which her crew could glimpse fleetingly before they plunged into the next cavernous trough.

The coaster lay to her starboard anchor in eight fathoms of water and was clearly on the move. Her engine was racing in impotent fury, trying to take some strain off the anchor cable. She was yawing some 90° and heavy seas were breaking clean over her, making impossible any attempt by her crew to get forward to let go the second anchor.

Rescued crewmembers from the coaster Hindlea *received tea and sympathy from the ladies of Moelfre after eight men were plucked to safety from certain death beneath the cliffs of Anglesey.*

INSET: Coxswain Richard Evans of Moelfre lifeboat is the last man to have been twice awarded the gold medal. The first came in 1959 with the Hindlea *rescue and the second in 1967 when fifteen men were saved from the Greek freighter* Nafsiporos.

The lifeboat and Hindlea *are between two 'snarling mountains of fury', as Dick Evans described the waves that day in 1959.*
One hundred years had passed since the hurricane that brought the Royal Charter *ashore, just a few hundred yards to the west.*

71

The northerly wind and the tide setting to the south-south-east both conspired to force the *Hindlea* towards the shore. For an hour and twenty-five minutes the lifeboat stood by, her crew watching the coaster's inexorable progress, knowing that the longer her skipper left the agonising decision to abandon ship, the more dangerous the eventual rescue operation would become.

At last, with his ship only 200 yards from the rocks, the captain gave the order to abandon ship. All eight men aboard her moved to a position lining the railings on the port side of the poop deck. The lifeboat, which had been keeping station head to sea on the starboard beam of the coaster all the time she was standing by, turned for the casualty.

There was precious little sea room between the *Hindlea*'s stern and the shore, but Coxswain Evans knew he would have to negotiate that treacherous gap if he were to make an approach on the lee side of the ship where the men had gathered. Close to the shore the sea had become not only rough but extremely confused, and as the lifeboat presented her starboard side to the weather to manoeuvre round the coaster's stern, she was hit by a tremendous breaking sea. Immediately she rolled over onto her beam ends, so far over, in fact, that her masts went under water.

Mercifully she came upright, just in time for her crew to catch sight of the *Hindlea*'s thrashing propeller high above their heads as their coxswain fought with the helm to steer round the coaster's stern, and to bring the lifeboat's head back into the wind and alongside the *Hindlea*'s port quarter.

One man on the ship saw his chance and jumped to the deck of the lifeboat. A crew-member grabbed him and Dick Evans went full astern, clear of the lethal propeller. The lifeboat then moved in again. This time the coaster had yawed

The crew of the Hindlea *are about to be snatched to safety. However, it took ten attempts to accomplish this.*

Moelfre lifeboat coxswain Richard Evans receives his RNLI gold medal, for the service to the Hindlea, *from HRH Princess Marina, Duchess of Kent, President of the RNLI from 1943 to 1968.*

The shattered remains of the Hindlea *soon after she was driven onto the rocks by 100mph winds.*

round so far that her port side was exposed to the full force of the hurricane. The waves, bigger than ever in the shallower water, lifted the lifeboat high up the side of the casualty so that the two vessels struck. The coxswain thought he was about to be deposited onto the *Hindlea*'s deck and that at very least he had seriously damaged his boat.

Fortunately the collision was not as serious at it could have been and the lifeboat withdrew in order to make another approach. This time the coxswain knew to wait until the coaster's stern had slewed round towards the east before he attempted to run in under the meagre amount of lee provided by the raised poop deck.

Ten times he successfully completed this perilous manoeuvre and each time except for two he came away with a single survivor. By the time the eighth and final man was aboard there was little more than a hundred yards between the

Hindlea and the rocks. In spite of the appalling conditions the rescue operation itself had taken barely sixteen minutes, such was the skill of the coxswain and crew. One of the rescued men had a broken ankle but the rest were found to be shaken but unscathed when the lifeboat put them ashore at 2.37pm, just over two and a half hours after she had set out. The abandoned *Hindlea* ran onto the rocks soon afterwards and broke up.

The gold medal for gallantry awarded to Coxswain Richard Evans following this rescue was not to be his last. Eight years later the Holyhead and Moelfre lifeboats between them rescued fifteen men from the Greek freighter *Nafsiporos* and Dick Evans was once again honoured with the gold medal for his bravery. For the *Hindlea* rescue the lifeboat's motor mechanic, Evan Owens, was awarded a silver medal and the rest of the crew were awarded the bronze medal.

16

RESCUE FROM THE *JOHAN COLLETT*

Off Guernsey, 5 February 1963

Gold Medal to Coxswain Hubert Petit, Guernsey

Carrying a cargo of zinc concentrates, the Norwegian merchant ship *Johan Collett* was steaming up the English Channel, bound for the Belgian river port of Ghent on the last leg of her journey from Tunis. It was 5 February 1963.

The weather had been getting worse with a near gale force 7 freshening all the time from the south. Fourteen miles west-north-west of Les Hanois lighthouse on the island of Guernsey her trouble started. At 3.15pm her skipper radioed for immediate help; his cargo had shifted and his vessel was listing severely to starboard.

At St Peter Port, Guernsey, the assembly signal for the lifeboat crew was made and by 3.45pm the 52ft Barnett class lifeboat, *Euphrosyne Kendal*, was free of her mooring and heading out of the harbour. Already the sea was rough as the wind strengthened; the skies were overcast and visibility only moderate.

Few men, if any, had better knowledge of Guernsey's treacherous shore than Coxswain Hubert Petit, in command of the lifeboat that afternoon. Immediately he put that knowledge to good use. Knowing time was of the essence and that a three-and-a-half-knot foul tide was running offshore, Hubert Petit set a course which hugged the south of the island. This meant keeping to within only fifty yards of the shore and actually passing inside the rocks which lined the coast. (Later, the coxswain was to praise two of his crew for the skilful navigational assistance they provided during this passage. One was his mechanic, Eric Pattimore, and the other his son, John Petit, who eventually succeeded him as coxswain in 1964.)

Coxswain Hubert Petit of St Peter Port, Guernsey, won the gold medal for rescuing six men from the Norwegian merchant ship Johan Collett *in storm force winds. His son, John, who was a crewmember on the same mission, became coxswain on his father's retirement. (Photograph by courtesy of the* Lion Annual.*)*

The lifeboat made excellent time, passing Les Hanois lighthouse at 4.46pm. But she still had nearly two hours' steaming before she would reach the casualty.

Other ships had also answered *Johan Collett*'s distress. The South African frigate, *President Kruger*, was on her way to help along with six other vessels. By 5pm the *SS Bonnard* was on the scene and the casualty's skipper decided he would lower the ship's boat while the weather still allowed him to do so. Eleven of his crew were thus transferred safely to the attendant vessel which was to land them eventually at Ostend.

An hour later three more men from the stricken merchant ship boarded a rubber life-raft and were picked up by the *SS Kaupanger*, another of the ships that by now were standing by. The arrival of the warship *President Kruger* allowed the remaining merchant ships to continue on their way.

At 6.30pm Guernsey lifeboat arrived on the scene. By now the wind had backed to the south-east and had strengthened to full gale force. It was snowing and ice was forming on the lifeboat's windscreen. Through it however the coxswain could make out the shape of the *Johan Collett* as she lay stopped in the water. She was wallowing, her port beam to the wind, in seas measuring some fifteen feet from trough to crest. She was listing heavily to starboard with her gunwale awash.

Her master had earlier decided to refuse a tow from the attendant warship and risk waiting for the arrival of a tug, *Abeille 10*, summoned from Cherbourg.

All the time the weather was getting worse. The lifeboat could only stand by, waiting for the next decision from the casualty's master. The only means by which Coxswain Petit could talk to him was via the *President Kruger* who relayed the lifeboat's RT signals by lamp. The mast-head signalling lamp on the lifeboat was useless as it was constantly disappearing from view while the lifeboat plunged deep into every trough.

Three hours the lifeboat waited, until at 9.35pm the *Johan Collett*'s master asked the lifeboat to take off his chief engineer and two apprentices. Coxswain Petit steered towards the starboard and lee quarter of the merchant ship. On his first run in he quickly realised that blocks and falls swinging free from the empty davits on the ship would imperil the whole operation and he shouted that they be hauled inboard.

He then made three further approaches. Each time he held his lifeboat alongside just long enough for a man to jump. That mission accomplished, he pulled away to stand by for further developments.

They came first of all in the form of the arrival of the aircraft carrier, *HMS Ark Royal*. Next on the scene came the tug, *Abeille 10*, at 10.41pm. In an operation which occupied the next hour and a half and seven attempts, the tug finally

Hubert Petit reconnoitres the weather side of the Johan Collett *before taking her crew from the stern. In the background the South African frigate* President Kruger *gives assistance with her searchlight.*

secured a tow-line to the *Johan Collett*. Slowly, at about three knots, she began towing into the wind. Immediately the casualty's list increased to some 40°.

The weather had reached its worst. A three-knot tide was running against the full force of the gale which was gusting to force 10 and creating very rough, steep seas. The *Johan Collett* was on her beam ends and seas were sweeping her port side.

Now, at 12.45am, came the decision to abandon ship. Somehow in those appalling conditions six men had to be taken off the vessel which was still being towed at three knots. Coxswain Petit began his first run in under the port quarter; his aim was to position the lifeboat's starboard side alongside the merchant ship while on the top of a sea and to stay there long enough for a man to jump.

Under illumination provided by the *President Kruger*'s searchlights the lifeboat made her approach. A huge sea picked up her bow and threw it off course. Hubert Petit regained control and prepared for a second run in. This time a survivor jumped on board and on the next approach two men made it over the lifeboat's rails. Another approach and another survivor was grabbed, but on the fifth attempt the man to jump hesitated for a second and he fell twenty feet into the lifeboat.

Only the master was left and the coxswain turned the lifeboat round for his sixth run in. When the time came to jump the man fell outside the lifeboat's guard-rail. Three of the lifeboat crew sprang forward and with all their strength dragged him inboard seconds before the two vessels struck one another heavily.

St Peter Port lifeboat now turned for home with nine survivors aboard. She eventually arrived at 6.45am, exactly fifteen hours after her launch.

Hubert Petit received the gold medal for gallantry following this rescue. His son John Petit and Motor Mechanic Eric Pattimore received the bronze medal.

St Peter Port lifeboat Euphrosyne Kendal *under the illumination of the searchlight of the South African frigate* President Kruger.

17

THE LOSS OF THE *LYRMA*

Off Start Point, 6 December 1976

Gold Medal to Second Coxswain Keith Bower, Torbay

The Devon coastline between Exmouth and Start Point runs very nearly due north to south. On the evening of Sunday, 5 December 1976, a southerly storm had been steadily brewing which by midnight had reached its full force and was causing steep forty-foot waves to push their way northwards against a one-knot tide along this stretch of coast.

Just before 1am on the sixth, Torbay lifeboat station received a call. A Panamanian cargo vessel, the *Lyrma*, was listing dangerously, her steering gear broken down, her radar not functioning and her position uncertain although she was thought to be six miles east of Start Point.

It took the seven-man lifeboat crew less than twenty minutes at that ungodly hour to receive the call, leave their bed, dress, reach the boat-house, put on their gear, board the lifeboat and speed out of Brixham harbour. One man who was not with them that night was their coxswain. He had been caught out at sea by the storm in his fishing boat and so it was the station's second coxswain, Keith Bower, who took the helm of the 54ft Arun class lifeboat, *Edward Bridges (Civil Service No. 37)*, as she steamed at her full nineteen knots towards Berry Head.

It was only when the lifeboat rounded the headland to turn southwards that the full force of the storm hit her. Keith Bower later recounted his experiences of that night and here takes up the story:

'We went round Berry Head and hit the first big sea, which was a total shock to me. We battened down and plotted the course down to the casualty. The wind was about south-south-west, about head to wind on the course we had to go. By this time we had hit three of these big seas and we were right in the teeth of it.

'We could hear the engines revving and dying as we left the tops of the crests and fell into the troughs. I estimated the boat to be airborne, practically, at times. Well, my brother, Stephen [the motor mechanic], he took off out of his seat and jammed his knees under the mechanic's desk. So for our own comfort and the safety of the ship we eased her down on the very big crests. You could actually see the white water coming over the bow, so we eased her down.'

Keith Bower also found that the lifeboat made marginally easier progress in the worsening weather by 'tacking', or steering with the wind first on the port bow then on the starboard bow. Few lifeboatmen are totally immune to seasickness and at least four of Keith Bower's crew that night were suffering its debilitating effects. They did not allow it to get in the way of their duties, however, even when poring over the chart, and peering at the radar screen as the lifeboat fell and rose and twisted in the mountainous seas.

They forged on southwards, still not knowing the exact whereabouts of the stricken *Lyrma*. At one point the lifeboat altered course towards a contact on the radar but it was soon seen to be making good progress northward and definitely not a ship with steering failure. At last, at 2.15am, the coastguard radioed through with an updated position for the casualty.

It meant another five miles' steaming for the lifeboat. When she finally arrived, her crew could make out the lights of three vessels: the *Lyrma*, the 27,000-ton *Eurofreighter* and another, smaller vessel standing by. The wind was still blowing at force 10 to 11 and even before he came close, Keith Bower saw his chances of effecting a rescue as so remote that he radioed for a Sea King helicopter.

As the lifeboat drew closer the *Lyrma*'s plight became more obvious. She had a very heavy list to starboard, and was slowly steaming in a circle to starboard, pitching and rolling so that her well-deck was awash each time she heeled dangerously back onto her starboard list. Her captain, who had only joined the ship ten days earlier and who was the only English speaker aboard, radioed that any further shift of cargo would capsize his ship. He wanted everyone taken off.

The conditions were getting even worse. The wind, as strong as ever, had shifted, confusing the very heavy swell and making it entirely unpredictable. Furthermore, no Sea King helicopter was available.

Clearly there was much confusion aboard the *Lyrma*. Nothing happened when Keith Bower told her captain to put his life-raft over the side and get his crew into it. This was the only method of rescue the coxswain believed had any chance of success.

Finally, a life-raft did appear in the water over the port side forward but no one seemed willing to get into it. By then it was known, too, that a Royal Fleet Auxiliary vessel, *Engadine*, was approaching with a Wessex helicopter aboard.

When the helicopter arrived a winchman was lowered over the freighter's aft superstructure. The pilot's instruments were showing that the *Lyrma*'s deck was rising and falling some 30 feet in the seas below. The man on the wire swung like a pendulum in the wind and a second approach had to be made. This time the wire became entangled with a boat's davit and the winchman, injured, had to be hoisted back into the helicopter. Keith Bower takes up the story again:

'The helicopter told us the job was impossible for him, unless the crew got into the liferaft. At that moment I had the feeling of helplessness. What the hell are we going to do? The helicopter can't do it. We can't do it without the possibility of serious damage to the lifeboat and the *Lyrma*.

'And then the captain left the wheel to go and do something, and the ship stayed broadside. Now this is an aspect he didn't want because he was afraid of a capsize. We could hear his cargo moving, smashing up and down. It was chipboard and diesel oil in drums. The diesel had soaked one lot of chipboard and it was getting heavy, so that he had extra weight to one side, thus causing the vessel to list.

'When he left the wheel, the *Lyrma* stayed bow in toward the shore and stern out to sea. We sat there, stopped in the water like a duck. Then I said, "I think maybe we would be able to get in on his starboard quarter."

'Anyway, we went in. I'm not sure whether we touched or not, but we got pretty close. I was surprised how quietly she went in and came out. We wouldn't have broken an egg, even in those conditions. I said to John [John Hunkin, the assistant mechanic], "I think we could have had one then," and he said, "Yes." So we asked the captain to muster the crew on the starboard side.'

With two crew members on the foredeck, the lifeboat made her first approach. A woman passenger was grabbed as the two vessels came together; one person saved, nine still to go. The next approach was abortive but the third brought two of the freighter's crew safely aboard. The fourth allowed only one more to be pulled to safety before the coxswain had to reverse out of danger and the fifth produced none at all.

On the sixth run in, the *Lyrma* chose that moment to roll heavily to starboard and the lifeboat found herself trapped under the casualty's gunwales. On the foredeck the lifeboat crewmen leapt for cover behind the pulpit rails as the guard-rails were bent to 45° and their bolts sheared with a sound like rifle shots.

Meanwhile in the upper steering position, John Hunkin, next to his coxswain, fended off with his hand one of the *Lyrma*'s lifeboats still in its davit, as it loomed menacingly over their heads. In the midst of the confusion a survivor jumped to the lifeboat's deck. Another hesitated, but was grabbed by one of the lifeboat crew who had left his position of comparative safety behind the pulpit rail to do so. Keith Bower chose his moment to put both engines full astern and to everyone's relief the lifeboat shrugged herself free.

Undaunted, the coxswain prepared for yet another approach. It was successful and a seventh person was saved. Now only the captain remained aboard and on the second attempt he, too, was taken off. The captain was not the last to be rescued, however. Two of the crew had decided to board the life-raft which was still attached to the *Lyrma*'s port bow while the lifeboat had been taking off their fellows. The two occupants were finally persuaded to cut the line which held them so that they could float down wind to the lifeboat. It was 4.10am when these last survivors were pulled to safety.

Visibility had improved slightly for the return journey to Brixham and the coxswain was able to stay at his upper steering position. This enabled him to keep an eye on the large seas which now followed the lifeboat home and thus take action to avoid broaching. Two broaches did occur, however, before the lifeboat was safely back in harbour. She had been at sea close on four hours.

While Acting Coxswain Keith Bower was awarded the gold medal for this rescue, his crew that night all received the bronze medal.

Second Coxswain Keith Bower, chaired by his crew, outside the Royal Festival Hall, London, on the day he was presented with the gold medal for his rescue of ten men from the Lyrma.

Coxswain Keith Bower arrives at the scene. Lyrma *is plunging into the swell and her propeller is breaking clear of the water and thrashing in the air. Gestures are made to the crew that a helicopter will first attempt a rescue.*

18

THE *REVI* RESCUE

Off the Humber, 14 February 1979

Gold Medal to Coxswain Brian Bevan, Humber

February; a north-easterly gale, gusting to force 9 and increasing; snowstorms; midnight. Difficult for any east coast lifeboatman to sleep easily when the weather is in that sort of mood at that time of year. The last thing they want is a call but somehow they expect one.

This is, in fact, 13 February 1979. Brian Bevan, full-time coxswain and superintendent of Humber lifeboat station is aroused three minutes before midnight by the coastguard. A small cargo vessel, the *Revi*, Panamanian registered and carrying silver sand from France to Newcastle, is in distress thirty miles north-east of Spurn lightvessel. Heavy seas have ripped away her hatch covers and water is entering her hold.

Eighteen minutes later and eight men, including the coxswain, are aboard the 54ft Arun class lifeboat, *City of Bradford IV*. She has slipped her mooring in the shelter of Spurn Point and is heading into the darkness out to sea at full speed.

The settlement at Spurn Point, where one of the busiest lifeboats in the country is stationed. The boathouse and slipway is no longer in use; instead, the Arun class lifeboat lies afloat on a mooring under the shelter of the headland. Her crew are the RNLI's only full-time lifeboatmen. (Photograph by courtesy of the Grimsby Evening Telegraph*).*

Now she is clear of the Humber, climbing and falling from mountainous head seas. The impact into the trough of one twenty-foot sea opens every electric breaker and plunges the wheelhouse into darkness. The coxswain reduces speed to fourteen knots, the waves increase, some as high as thirty-five feet.

Fifty minutes of gruelling progress have been made by the lifeboat when the *Revi* puts out an even more urgent distress: she is now slowly sinking. She requests the British ship *Deepstone*, which is already standing by, to stand in close to. The lifeboat still has eight miles to run.

The lifeboat crew get their first glimpse of the casualty at 1.36am. Her master, in a desperate attempt to make the River Humber, is steaming at full speed towards them, his ship continually buried by the huge seas. The wind is at storm force 10 as the lifeboat takes up station close astern of the *Revi*.

A few minutes pass, then the master radios that he is slowing down. He wants two crew-members taken off. Coxswain Bevan asks him to stop so that he can work out the best way to carry out this apparently impossible request. He tells the master to steer south at slow speed and to have the two men on the boat deck on her starboard quarter, ready to jump.

Brian Bevan rams the throttles full astern as a huge wave threatens to engulf lifeboat, casualty and all on the Revi.
The forecastle of the Revi *is submerged, her cargo of silver sand is waterlogged, and her well-deck is awash.*

81

Two crew are ready to jump, and are illuminated in the beam of light from the lifeboat's bridge.

RIGHT: The men responsible for saving the Revi's crew: (left to right) Crew Member Dennis Bailey jun., Crew Member Peter Jordan, Motor Mechanic Bill Sayers, Superintendent Coxswain Brian Bevan, Second Coxswain Dennis Bailey, Crew Member Sydney Rollinson, Assistant Mechanic Ronald Sayers and Crew Member Michael Storey. (Photograph by courtesy of T. M. Carter.)

FAR RIGHT: A case of déjà vu: Brian Bevan goes up for the third time, to receive the gold medal from the RNLI President, HRH The Duke of Kent, at the 1979 annual awards ceremony. Bevan is the only man to have been awarded a bronze, silver and gold medal for bravery all at the same ceremony. (Photograph by courtesy of Peter Hadfield.)

Then the lifeboat moves in, fendered on the port quarter and her crew ready on the foredeck, their lifelines secure. The lifeboat edges in under the casualty's starboard quarter and a huge wave crashes over the port quarter, completely engulfing the coaster's stern.

Brian Bevan throttles full astern just in time to see *Revi*'s bulk fall back down, missing his foredeck by inches. Again and again the lifeboat makes an approach and is forced back, the casualty often towering twenty feet above the heads of the men on the foredeck. At last the right moment comes and the two crewmen are able to throw themselves into the waiting arms of the lifeboatmen.

With two of his men safe, *Revi*'s skipper hopes to continue the desperate run for the River Humber, but it is not to be. Only five minutes pass before the accommodation begins to flood, the cargo of sand shifts and the ship is listing 45° to port. Now he and the mate must abandon ship.

His final act at the helm is to turn the bow to the west to give a lee on the low port side. Meanwhile the lifeboat crew are fighting to secure fenders, this time to the starboard side, and to make themselves fast to the pulpit rails. The *Revi* is clearly sinking, she is down by the head and seas are sweeping clear across her full length.

A massive sea breaking clean over both vessels forces the lifeboat contemptuously away from the side of the casualty as Brian Bevan makes his first approach. Unflinching he comes in again, another thunderous wave hurls the lifeboat aside. Only on the twelfth attempt does the sea provide sufficient respite for the mate to jump six feet from his position on the ship's port quarter. He lands in the arms of the lifeboat crew who break his fall and hurry him below.

The *Revi* is now at a crazy angle; her bow is below the waves and her stern juts clear of the water, menacing the lifeboat with a lethal blow if she dares to come close. Her master is praying that the coxswain will dare. He is hanging on for dear life to the outside of the stern rails, ready to jump. Nine times the lifeboat gets close but not close enough. On the tenth the stricken vessel's stern soars twenty feet clear of the water and then plummets towards the lifeboat's foredeck and the crew immediately beneath.

Only the coxswain's lightning reaction – ramming the throttles full astern – and the power of the Arun class engines avert a total tragedy, literally by inches. Then three successive seas cover the *Revi* completely. The lifeboat crew cannot believe their eyes as the water clears and the captain is still seen hanging onto the stern rails.

But the ship is about to roll over. Bevan decides on a dash in to the casualty in a trough between two waves. The lifeboat drives in under the port quarter, strikes the stern, but the captain is able to jump. He lands on the very edge of the lifeboat's deck and is only prevented from being lost overboard by the strong arms of the crew. Five minutes later the *Revi* rolls over and sinks.

Besides the gold medal awarded to Coxswain Brian Bevan, his entire crew consisting of Second Coxswain Dennis Bailey, Motor Mechanic Barry 'Bill' Sayers, Assistant Mechanic Ronald Sayers and Crew Members Michael Storey, Peter Jordan, Sydney Rollinson and Dennis Bailey Jnr, were awarded the RNLI's bronze medal for gallantry.

Brian Bevan in fact made history when he attended the RNLI annual presentation of awards in London in May 1979. He was the first man to receive a bronze, silver and gold medal, all won within a year and all presented at the same ceremony.

19

TWENTY-NINE RESCUED FROM THE *BONITA*

Mid-Channel, 13 December 1981

Gold Medal to Coxswain Michael Scales, Guernsey

The English Channel was no place to be on Sunday, 13 December 1981. A southerly force 10 with gusts reaching hurricane force 12 had whipped the sea into a fury and was herding mountainous waves, breaking at their crests, across the shipping lanes of the south-west approaches.

It was not long before the storm began to take its toll. Even in the shelter of St Peter Port harbour a vessel had broken adrift and the Guernsey lifeboat crew had been summoned from their Sunday lunch to ensure the lifeboat was not damaged at her mooring. She was the 52ft Arun class *Sir William Arnold*, one of only three of her class to be built in wood, and the pride and joy of the station.

While they were aboard a message came through that an Ecuadorean cargo ship, the *Bonita*, was in distress. A Danish motor vessel, the *Charlottenburg*, had relayed the Mayday to St Peter Port, adding that she was steaming to the assistance of the freighter which had developed a 40° list to starboard. There were thirty-six people aboard her, including women and children.

Torbay lifeboat station on the Devon coast was marginally closer to the *Bonita*'s reported mid-Channel position than St Peter Port but she was already on service to a yacht.

Therefore, at exactly 2pm Guernsey lifeboat slipped her moorings and headed out into an ordeal which was to last nine hours in conditions her coxswain, Michael Scales, had never before experienced and would never be likely to again.

He had not only to contend with gusts of hurricane force and an extremely rough sea, but driving snow and spray which reduced visibility to 200 yards. The snow also had the effect of blanking out the radar which meant all navigation had to be done by the Decca radio navigation system.

As the lifeboat headed northwards up the east coast of Guernsey, huge following seas rose up at the stern, and as each one picked her up she would surge forward at a crazy downhill angle while the coxswain fought to retain control at the helm, keeping her head forward.

Bonita *with a list of 45° to starboard is attended by Sea King helicopters.*

Then the first broaching occurred; the lifeboat's stern rose to another sea, but this time there was nothing Michael Scales could do to prevent his boat being slewed round at right-angles to her course and rolling violently as she came broadside on to the weather. Immediately Scales swung the helm back on course and throttled forward under full power to regain control.

For two and a half hours the lifeboat drove on before the storm and in that time survived no fewer than seven further broachings. At last, some 30 miles out into the channel, in the dusk of the December afternoon, the lifeboat crew could make out the shape of the *Bonita*.

Her list was now 45° to starboard, presenting her high side to the wind. Some seas were sweeping right over her decks and she rolled heavily. She was so far over that the guard-rails on the lee side were submerged, as was the starboard wing of her bridge. The coxswain also noticed that ropes, drums and large pieces of timber were floating in the water, trapped on the lee side.

The lifeboat was not alone with the *Bonita*, however. Four other large vessels were standing as close as they dared and two helicopters were hovering nearby. In fact, a Sea King from RNAS Culdrose had earlier, in daylight, lifted four people off and landed them on the mainland. Since then, all attempts at helicopter rescue had failed.

The lifeboat made its approach. It was soon obvious to Michael Scales that his only chance of taking survivors off was to run in to the *Bonita*'s transom, so he indicated to the group of people huddled together on the steeply sloping deck to make their way aft. The first man to move fell and broke his leg. His companions could do no more than lash him to the hatch which would at least prevent his being washed overboard. They all then began to scramble along the outside of the ship's rails towards the stern.

When they got there they were faced with the alarming sight of the lifeboat, one moment high on the top of a wave, level with the after deck, and the next

The St Peter Port lifeboat Sir William Arnold, *running at full throttle before the storm, arrives at the scene to see two Sea King helicopters hovering over the* Bonita *which has a 45° list to starboard.*

plunging out of sight fifty feet down in the trough. As the lifeboat reached the bottom of her fall, the *Bonita*'s rudder loomed above the men on the deck, threatening a devastating blow as the next wave carried her back up.

To avoid the rudder, Michael Scales ran in at an angle, presenting his port side to the transom. Three men jumped but they timed it wrongly and fell some twenty-five feet to the deck. One of them landed on the stanchions and deckhouse and received appalling injuries from which he would later die. Meanwhile, the lifeboat was being swept round the ship's stern to where the floating debris lay. Using the starboard engine, furthest from the lethal flotsam, the coxswain managed to coax the lifeboat clear without fouling his propellers.

A different method of approach was needed. This time the lifeboat drew up to the transom and when she was only four feet away Second Coxswain Peter Bougourd hurled the heaving line aboard *Bonita*. It was held, and while the coxswain struggled to keep the lifeboat from being swept either among the debris or high onto the casualty's deck, two women managed to get the heaving line around them.

With considerable courage they then both leapt from the ship's stern into the sea. Scales put the lifeboat gently astern until he was two boat-lengths away from the ship and the women were hauled aboard.

The next three survivors were rescued using the same method, although two of them, losing their grip of the line when they were in the water, had to swim clear of the debris before the lifeboat crew could pull them aboard.

The wind, which all the time had maintained a steady violent storm force 11, creating 45 to 50 foot waves, chose this moment to shift round to the north-west and, if anything, increase in strength. The seas at the *Bonita*'s stern became extremely confused. Still the rescue by heaving line continued. At one point, as the lifeboat crew were engaged in pulling a survivor from the sea, another man fell from the ship's stern. He was not wearing a life-jacket and was immediately swept into the debris and down the starboard side of the casualty.

The lifeboat chased after him but when the attendant *Charlottenburg* reported that he appeared to be dead in the water, Michael Scales made the agonising decision to return to the survivors he knew he still had a chance of saving.

Not every approach he made to the casualty ended in success. Sometimes the engines had to be put abruptly astern to avoid a collision. On one occasion both engines failed momentarily at the precise moment of escape. The lifeboat's bow became entrapped under the hull beneath the *Bonita*'s transom until the engines took up again and pulled her clear. Peter Bougourd in the bow with the heaving line missed being crushed by inches.

Coxswain Michael Scales pictured with the Guernsey lifeboat, Sir William Arnold, *in which he endured force 11 winds and 50 foot waves to rescue twenty-nine people from the cargo ship* Bonita. (Photograph by courtesy of Brian J. Green.)

After fifty runs in, sixteen people had been taken aboard the lifeboat. The crew needed a breather and a chance to restore their circulation after the freezing temperature and constant heavy spray. Coxswain Scales took the lifeboat upwind of the casualty for a few minutes before returning once more to his unenviable task.

During the respite, a helicopter made several attempted rescues and succeeded in lifting off one man.

Reaching what must have been the limits of their strength and endurance, as seas frequently engulfed them, the lifeboat crew continued to haul a further thirteen survivors aboard. One was all but drowned when they got him to the deck but prompt action to expel water from his lungs saved him. The thirteenth was the captain, who said he was the last man save the crew-member who could not be moved with his broken leg.

Another agonising decision now had to be made by the coxswain. Stay on the scene on behalf of this last man or make for Brixham and land the survivors already on board, including one in a critical condition? News coming through helped him to make up his mind. The helicopter, having left to refuel, was now on its way back and would try to get to the one remaining man aboard *Bonita*. Torbay lifeboat was also now making for the scene. Coxswain Scales set a course for Brixham and headed off into what had become the teeth of the gale. After

falling into a deep trough in the massive head seas, the lifeboat had to continue at reduced speed to prevent further injury to the survivors aboard.

St Peter Port lifeboat finally entered harbour on the Devon coast at 11.13pm and disembarked her twenty-nine survivors. Her shattered crew were relieved to hear that the man they had been forced to abandon aboard the *Bonita* had been rescued. The skipper of a French tug, the *Abeille Languedoc*, which had been standing by, noticed that the man had slipped from his position on the stern hatch cover and, after hanging on for a while, had slipped into the sea. Torbay lifeboat had not yet arrived so the tug moved in rapidly and rescued him from the water. The *Bonita* herself sank early the next day.

Besides the RNLI's gold medal which was awarded to Coxswain Michael Scales, the bronze medal was presented to each of his seven crew members.

Two gold medals were awarded at the RNLI's 1982 presentation ceremony. One was to Michael Scales (right) for the Bonita *rescue, the other was a posthumous award to Trevelyan Richards, the coxswain of Penlee lifeboat who, together with his crew, lost his life trying to save those aboard the ill-fated coaster* Union Star. *Coxswain Richards' mother Mary is pictured here, having received her son's medal.* (Photograph by courtesy of the Guernsey Press Co. Ltd.)

20

THE PENLEE TRAGEDY

19 December 1981

Gold Medal to Coxswain Trevelyan Richards

Coxswain Trevelyan Richards.

The tragedy which befell the Penlee lifeboat six days before Christmas 1981, when all eight of her crew were lost together with the eight people they were attempting to save, had a profound and lasting effect on the RNLI and the British public at large. The shock and grief it caused in a small Cornish community is remembered to this day even by people who otherwise have had little involvement in the lifeboat service and who live nowhere near the sea.

The story is told here, not only because a gold medal was won in the rescue attempt, but also to show just how real are the risks lifeboatmen sometimes have to take and how dire the consequences when courage is not repaid by good fortune.

With no one surviving to tell the tale, details of precisely what happened on the night of 19 December are understandably scarce, but with the help of recorded messages to the coastguard and the eyewitness accounts of a Royal Naval helicopter pilot and a salvage tug skipper, a story of immense courage does emerge. It is told succinctly but movingly in the pages of the *Lifeboat* journal of the day:

'Penlee lifeboat, the 47ft Watson class *Solomon Browne*, with her coxswain, Trevelyan Richards, and all on board, was lost on the night of Saturday December 19 during a service to the 1,400 ton coaster *Union Star*, registered in Dublin.

'*Solomon Browne* had launched in a violent storm to go to the aid of *Union Star* which had reported engine failure when eight miles east of Wolf Rock Lighthouse and which was drifting rapidly on to the cliffs four miles south-west of Penlee lifeboat station; there were eight people on board, including one woman and two teenage girls. The weather was atrocious. The wind, blowing from south by east, increased to hurricane force 12, gusting to 90 knots; there was a heavy ground swell and the mountainous seas were reported to be 60ft high; in driving rain, visibility was very poor. So bad were the conditions that in spite of many attempts a Royal Navy Sea King helicopter, piloted by Lt-Cdr Russell L. Smith, USN, was unable to lift off any of the coaster's crew.

'Coxswain Richards repeatedly took his lifeboat alongside the coaster in these appalling conditions to try to rescue the eight people on board. Latterly on at least two occasions the lifeboat was lifted by a huge wave onto the deck of the *Union Star*, then sliding stern first back into the sea. Subsequently, Coxswain Richards drove her alongside once more and four people on the deck jumped into the lifeboat. The *Solomon Browne* was observed to have slammed hard against the coaster's side but was seen moving away, apparently still under control.

'The last radio message from the lifeboat confirmed that four people had been rescued and before returning to their base the helicopter crew saw *Solomon Browne*, then only about 50 yards off the steep and rocky shore, turn, possibly to make another approach. There was no further radio contact with the lifeboat, but her lights were seen to disappear some ten minutes later, at about the same time that *Union Star* was overwhelmed and laid on her side to the west of Tater-du Lighthouse.

'Despite many hours search through the night and the following day by the St Mary's, Isle of Scilly, and the Lizard-Cadgwith lifeboats, by helicopters, by HM Coastguard coast rescue teams and by fishing vessels, no survivors were recovered from either *Solomon Browne* or *Union Star*.'

No-one survived the wreck of the Union Star. *This is how the coaster appeared when dawn broke, following the tragedy of the night before at the foot of the cliffs close to Tater-du Light.*

'We've got four off . . . just going in for the remainder.' Trevelyan Richards turns the Solomon Browne *back to rescue the four people left on board the* Union Star. *What could be an empty life jacket is illuminated in the dark water by the searchlight beam. The masts and light of the salvage tug* Noord Holland *show above the foredeck of the* Union Star.

89

To this day no one knows for sure how the lifeboat met her end. By the wreckage which was found afterwards it was clear that somehow she had been smashed to smithereens by some enormous impact. Whether it was the sea hurling her onto the jagged rocks where the *Union Star* had run aground or the effects of her being crushed by the capsizing coaster is impossible to deduce. Whatever the cause, there is no doubt that the lifeboat coxswain had pursued his increasingly impossible mission to the end and that on this occasion the sea had proved itself to be the ultimate master.

The courage required by Trevelyan Richards to carry out the successful part of the rescue attempt when four people were taken off was enough to earn him the RNLI gold medal posthumously. His crew consisting of Second Coxswain/ Mechanic James Madron, Assistant Mechanic Nigel Brockman, Emergency Mechanic John Blewett and Crew Members Charles Greenhaugh, Kevin Smith, Barrie Torrie and Gary Wallis were all posthumously awarded the bronze medal for gallantry.

Following the public inquiry into the disaster R.F. Stone Esq. QC, the chairman, commented in his summing up:

'The loss of the *RNLB Solomon Browne* and her crew was caused ... in consequence of the persistent and heroic endeavours by the coxswain and his crew to save the lives of all from the *Union Star*. Such heroism enhances the highest traditions of the Royal National Lifeboat Institution in whose service they gave their lives.'

'Whatever the cause, there is no doubt that the lifeboat coxswain had pursued his increasingly impossible mission to the end and that on this occasion the sea had proved itself to be the ultimate master.' The Union Star *at her resting place in Lamorna Bay. (Photograph by courtesy of P. J. Packenas.)*

THE *JOHN AND JESSIE*
Wrecked off Holy Island, Northumberland, 30 October 1825

A violent gale sent the sloop *John and Jessie* running for Holy Island in distress. But at 10am, while attempting to cross the bar, she was wrecked on the shore. The heavy breakers immediately washed four young ladies, the master and one seaman to their deaths. Soon only the top half of the mast remained above water, with three desperate survivors clinging to it for dear life. A hundred people had gathered on the shore, but none had the initiative to help – until the resourceful McGeorge Joy, master of a revenue cutter, arrived on the beach.

He organised his own crew and men from a fishing smack to bring a fishing coble overland close to where the wreck lay. Together with four of his men, a fisherman and a pilot he launched into the surf and driving sleet. Several times they were driven back with the boat full of water, but at last they reached the survivors and pulled them to safety, only moments before the mast was washed away. The gold medal was awarded to McGeorge Joy.

The three remaining seamen cling to the mast of the sunken John and Jessie. *Joy approaches from Holy Island in his coble.*

RNLI GOLD MEDAL AWARDS
FOR GALLANTRY

Recipient	Casualty and Station		Date of Rescue
Fremantle, Capt C.H., RN*	Swedish Brig	Christchurch	8 March 1824
Clarke, Lt J., RN	Brig *Juno*	Biring Gap	8 Nov 1824
Benett, Capt C.C., RN	Brig *Unity*	Lyme Regis	23 Nov 1824
Granby, Lt S., RN*	Transport Ship *Admiral Berkeley*	Portsmouth	23 Nov 1824
Peake, Capt T., RN*	Transport Ship *Admiral Berkeley*	Portsmouth	23 Nov 1824
St Croix, P. de*	*Fanny* of St Malo	Jersey	9 Jan 1825
St Croix, F. de*	*Fanny* of St Malo	Jersey	9 Jan 1825
St Croix, J. de*	*Fanny* of St Malo	Jersey	9 Jan 1825
Randall, Lt H., RN	*Devoran*	Aberdeen	17 Jan 1825
Joy, G.*	Sloop *John and Jessie*	Holy Island	30 Oct 1825
Morris, Capt J.R., RN	Barque *Richard Pope*	Dundrum Bay, N.I.	6 March 1826
Else, Lt J., RN*	Sean Boat *Providence*	Fowey	26 Aug 1826
Bowen, Lt C.H., RN	*Rose* of Wick	Fraserburgh	2 Jan 1827
Lindsay, Lt J., RN	Sloop *Lively*	Fort George	2 Jan 1827
Jobson, Lt C., RN	*Clyde Packet*	Arbroath	17 Feb 1827
Jobson, Lt C., RN*	*Alice* of Sunderland	Arbroath	8 March 1827
Blois, Capt J.R., RN	Steam Packet *Venus*	Glynn, Co Wexford	18 March 1828
Matthews, Lt. R.B., RN	*Lord Duncan*	Lowestoft	12 Oct 1827
Hillary, Sir William, Bart	*Fortroendert* of Sweden	Douglas, IoM	10 Dec 1827
Broad, W.	Brig *Larch*	Falmouth	7 Jan 1828
Brunton, Lt J., RN	Schooner *Triton*	Newton-by-the-Sea	1 Dec 1828
		Northumberland	
Lingard, Lt J., RN	Brig *Henry*	Robin Hood's Bay	1 Dec 1828
	Brig *Esther*	Robin Hood's Bay	28 April 1829
Lloyd, Lt S., RN	Brig *Capricho* of Spain	Ballycotton	25 Jan 1829
Pym, Lt R.E., RN	Brig *Aurora*	Redcar	14 Aug 1829
Hutchison, Lt W., RN	Brig *Duke*	Dun Laoghaire	14 Aug 1829
Graham, Capt P., RN	Brig *Mountaineer*	Walmer	24 Nov 1829
Johnson, Lt W., RN	Brig *Mountaineer*	Walmer	24 Nov 1829
Watts, Lt S., RN	Brig *Mountaineer*	Walmer	24 Nov 1829
Hillary, Sir William, Bart	Sloop *Eclipse* of Glasgow	Douglas	14 Jan 1830
Jones, Lt R., RN	Brig *Smalls*	Whitby	18 Jan 1830
Prattent, Lt J., RN*	Lugger *La Constance* of France	Hastings	19 Jan 1830
James, Lt H., RN*	Lugger *La Constance* of France	Hastings	19 Jan 1830

Recipient	Casualty and Station		Date of Rescue
Hillary, Sir William, Bart*	RMS *St George*	Douglas	20 Nov 1830
Robinson, Lt R., RN*	RMS *St George*	Douglas	20 Nov 1830
Leigh, Lt T., RN	Brig *Henry*	Winterton	24 Dec 1839
	Collier Brig *Annabella*	Winterton	26 Nov 1830
James, W.	Brig *Le Bon Père* of France	Falmouth	6 Dec 1830
Jones, Lt R., RN	Sloop *Northfield*	Whitby	12 Dec 1830
Earle, Lt E.C., RN	Brig *Fame*	Rye	1 Feb 1831
Steane, Lt J., RN	Brig *Fame*	Rye	1 Feb 1831
Turner, Lt C., RN	Sloop *Janet*	Fraserburgh	5 May 1831
Parry, Lt H.L., RN	Fishing Boat *L'Aimée* of France	Rye	21 Nov 1831
Randall, Lt H., RN	Schooner *Wanderer*	Elie, Fife	2 Feb 1833
Leigh, Lt T., RN	*Crauford Davison*	Winterton	19 March 1833
Sumner, R.*	Pilot Boat *Good Intent*	Liverpool	29 Nov 1833
Snell, Lt G., RN	Brig *Pioneer*	Rye	24 Jan 1834
Williams, Rev J.	Smack *Active* of Belfast	Ramsey, IoM	7 March 1835
Owen, W.	*Plutarch* of USA	Holyhead	10 Sept 1835
Somerville, Lt J., RN	Brig *Industry*	Littlestone	2 Oct 1835
Cox, Lt. H., RN	Schooner *Tid* of Dundee	St Andrews	4 Oct 1835
Jellard, J.	*Francis Spaght*	Mid Atlantic	22 Dec 1835
Walsh, M.	*Glasgow* of USA	Wexford	15 Feb 1837
Essell, Lt W., RN	Sloop *Ann and Elizabeth*	Wexford	? Feb 1838
Hoed, Capt F.	*Columbia* of Liverpool	Azores	28 Jan 1838
Stark, Lt P., RN	Schooner *Ranger* of Perth	Broughty Ferry	4 March 1838
Rymer, Lt D., RN	Schooner *Margaret* of Dundee	Berwick-	8 April 1838
		upon-Tweed	
Browne, P.	Schooner *Bloom*	Dundrum Bay, N.I.	23 Oct 1838
Brittain, Lt G., RN	Brig *Jupiter* of Whitby	Whitby	29 Oct 1838
Lett, Lt S., RN	*Ariadne*	Wexford	25 Nov 1838
Ross, Capt T., RN	Brig *Gainsborough*	Malahide, Nr Dublin	29 Nov 1838
Symmes, Lt H., RN*	Brig *Claire* of France	Brook, IoW	29 Nov 1838
Thompson, R.	Schooner *Minerva*	Drogheda, Co Louth	31 March 1839
Collins, Capt J.*	Timber Ship *Scotia*	Mid Atlantic	5 Dec 1839
Metherell, Lt R., RN	Brig *Medora*	Youghal	23 Feb 1840
Sewell, Lt H., RN	Smack *Sarah*	Dundrum Bay, IoW	21 Sept 1840

Recipient	Casualty and Station		Date of Rescue
Macnamara, Lt T., RN	Brig *Victoria*, and Sloop *Lively*	Littlehampton	13 Nov 1840
Marsh, Capt D., RN	Three Boats	Brighton	13 Dec 1840
Steel, C.*	Steam Packet *Thames*	Isles of Scilly	4 Jan 1841
Quadling, B.	Brig *Latona*	Courtmacsherry	7 Feb 1842
Vicary, Lt W., RN	Brig *George*	Atherfield, IoW	14 Jan 1843
Bulley, Lt J., RN	Brig *George*	Atherfield, IoW	14 Jan 1843
Britton, Capt J.	*Dorchester*	Mid Atlantic	15 Sept 1844
Bulley, Lt J., RN	*Llan Rumney*	Atherfield, IoW	30 Dec 1847
Goss, Lt T., RN	*Mountaineer*	Dunmanus Bay, Co Cork	15 Dec 1850
Davies, Capt G., RN*	Brig *New Commercial* of Whitby	Penzance	12 Jan 1851
Forward, T.*	Brig *New Commercial* of Whitby	Penzance	12 Jan 1851
Ludlow, Capt I.	Emigrant Ship *Meridian*	Indian Ocean	23 Aug 1853
Hamilton, H.	Brig *Tregiste* of Trieste	Balbriggan	17 Nov 1858
Rodgers, J.*	SS *Royal Charter*	Moelfre	26 Oct 1859
Cobb, MA, Rev C.	Lugger *Courrier de Dieppe*	Dymchurch	6 Jan 1867
Elyard, Major J.	Schooner *Lion* of Goole	Broadstairs	12 March 1876
Cubitt, W., Jnr	Schooner *Richard Warbrick*	Bacton	20 Jan 1880
Torrens, Lt J.	Schooner *Robert Brown*	Dublin Bay	28 Oct 1880
Fish, C.*	Barque *Indian Chief*	Ramsgate	6 Jan 1881
Fish, C.	On retirement as Ramsgate Coxswain out on 353 services in 26 years, saved 877.		8 Oct 1891
McCombie, T.	Barque *Palme* of Finland		25 Dec 1895
Haylett, J.	Capsize of Caister Lifeboat		13 Nov 1901
Rees, D.	Yacht *Firefly*	Penarth	16 June 1907
Owen, W.*	SS *Harold* of Liverpool	Holyhead	22 Feb 1908
O'Shea, Rev J.	Schooner *Teaser* of Montrose	Ardmore	18 March 1911
Langlands, T.*	Hospital Ship *Rohilla*	Whitby	30 Oct 1914
Smith, R.*	Hospital Ship *Rohilla*	Whitby	30 Oct 1914

Recipient	Casualty and Station		Date of Rescue
Burton, Capt H.R.E.*	Hospital Ship *Rohilla*	Whitby	30 Oct 1914
Blogg, H.*	SS *Fernebo* of Sweden	Cromer	9 Jan 1917
Howells, J.	Schooner *Hermina*	Fishguard	3 Dec 1920
Swan, J.	SS *Hopelyn* of Newcastle	Lowestoft	20 Oct 1922
Fleming, W.	SS *Hopelyn* of Newcastle	Gorleston	20 Oct 1922
Jones, Capt O.	Ketch *Excel* of Poole	Moelfre	28 Oct 1927
Roberts, W.	Ketch *Excel* of Poole	Moelfre	28 Oct 1927
Blogg, H.	Tanker *Georgia* of Netherlands	Cromer	21 Nov 1927
Patton, R. (Posthumous)	Salvage Steamer *Disperser*	Runswick	8 Feb 1934
Sliney, P.*	Daunt Rock Lightship	Ballycotton	11 Feb 1936
Cross, R.*	Trawler *Gurth* of Grimsby	Humber	12 Feb 1940
Boyle, J.*	SS *Stolkwijk* of Netherlands	Arranmore	7 Dec 1940
Blogg, H.	Four Vessels	Cromer	6 Aug 1941
Murphy, P.*	SS *Browning* of Liverpool	Newcastle, Co Down	21 Jan 1942
McLean, J.*	SS's *Runswick* and *Saltwick*	Peterhead	23 Jan 1942
Bennison, Lt W., RNVR	SS *Hawkwood* of London	Hartlepool	26 Jan 1942
Cross, R.	HM Trawler *Almondine*	Humber	7 Jan 1943
Gammon, W.*	HMCS *Chebogue* of Canada	Mumbles	11 Oct 1944
King, T.*	Yacht *Maurice Georges* of Jersey	St Helier	13 Sept 1949
Evans, R.*	Cargo Vessel *Hindlea* of Cardiff	Moelfre	27 Oct 1959
Petit, H.*	CV *Johan Collett* of Norway	St Peter Port	5 Feb 1963
Harvey, L Cdr H., VRD RNR	CV *Nafsiporos* of Greece	Holyhead	2 Dec 1966
Evans, R.	CV *Nafsiporos* of Greece	Moelfre	2 Dec 1966
Bower, K.*	CV *Lyrma* of Panama	Torbay	6 Dec 1976
Bevan, B.*	CV *Revi* of Panama	Humber	14 Feb 1979
Scales, M.*	CV *Bonita* of Ecuador	St Peter Port	13 Feb 1981
Richards, W. (Posthumous)*	CV *Union Star* of Dublin	Penlee	19 Dec 1981

*Featured in this volume.

The RNLI also occasionally awards the gold medal for achievements other than outstanding bravery.

Sister lifeboat organisations in other countries often receive the RNLI gold medal to mark their centenary and in early years the RNLI presented the medal to individuals who had given outstanding service to the Institution in areas other than actual rescues.

The total of gold medals awarded in categories other than for bravery number 27.

BIBLIOGRAPHY

Beatty, John. *Lifeboats to the Rescue* (David & Charles, 1980)

Blampied, Guy. *Mayday! Mayday! A History of the Guernsey Lifeboat Station*

Farr, Grahame. Archives, RNLI, Poole

Farr, Grahame. *Wreck and Rescue in The Bristol Channel – Part II — The Story of the Welsh Lifeboats* (D. Bradford Barton Ltd, 1967)

Farr, Grahame and Noall, Cyril. *Wreck and Rescue Round the Cornish Coast – Part I — The Story of the North Coast Lifeboats* (D. Bradford Barton Ltd, 1964)

Howarth, Patrick. *The Lifeboat Story* (Routledge, Kegan, Paul, 1957)

Jolly, Cyril. *Henry Blogg of Cromer* (Cyril Jolly, 1958)

Kelly, Robert. *For Those in Peril* (Shearwater Press, 1979)

Kipling, Ray. *Rescue by Sail and Oar* (Topsail Books, 1982)

McKee, Alexander. *The Golden Wreck* (Souvenir Press, 1961)

Moignard, Ian G. *The History of Jersey's Lifeboats* (Ashton and Denton Publishing Co (CI) Ltd, 1975)

Morris, Jeff. Various Station History Booklets

Parry, Henry. *Wreck and Rescue on the Coast of Wales — Part II – The Story of the North Wales Lifeboats* (D. Bradford Barton Ltd, 1973)

Quiller-Couch, Sir Arthur. *The Story of the Sea* (1895)

Royal National Lifeboat Institution. *Archives*

Royal National Lifeboat Institution. The *Lifeboat* Journal

Skidmore, Ian. *Anglesey and Lleyn Shipwrecks* (Christopher Davies, 1979)

Skidmore, Ian. *Lifeboat VC* (David & Charles, 1979)

Smith, Carl. *The Men of The Mumbles Head* (Gomer Press, 1977)

Vince, Charles. *Storm on the Waters* (Hodder & Stoughton, 1946)

Warner, Oliver. *The Lifeboat Service* (Cassell, 1974)

Williams, R.R. *Anglesey and the Loss of the* Royal Charter (Anglesey Antiquarian Society and Field Club, 1959)

ACKNOWLEDGEMENTS

I wish to thank the following for their help and assistance in the conception and creation of this book:

Barry Cox (honorary librarian – RNLI); Capt J. Petit (Guernsey RNLI); B. Bevan (Spt Cox'n RNLI Hull); R.J. Atkinson, Hell Bay Hotel, Scilly Islands; Ian Denton, Tavistock (World Ship Society); Brian Ayres; Dick and Nancy Evans (Moelfre RNLI); D. Blackhurst, Salcombe; P.B. Mimmack (Assistant Harbourmaster, Jersey); Claude Dreager (*Anthése* Publishing, Paris); Capt T.A. Spencer (Harbourmaster, States Harbour Office, Guernsey); Trevor Burrows Photography, Plymouth; H.S. Appleyard, Cleveland (World Ship Society); W.M. Benn, Exmouth (World Ship Society); Martin Benn, Preston (World Ship Society); Keith Bower, Cox'n Retired, Torbay RNLI; J.J. Colledge, Wanstead (World Ship Society); Dr J. de Courcy Ireland, Dublin; S.J. Woodroffe (RNLI, Poole); Faith Glasgow; Alison Elks, David & Charles; Martin Harrop, Eyemouth; Norman Hooke, Lloyds Maritime Information Services; B. Lawley, Manchester; C.G. Laidlaw, General Register & Record Office of Shipping, Cardiff; J.L. Loughran, Solihull (World Ship Society); National Maritime Museum (R.G. Todd); Cliff Parsons, Manchester; Gordon Read National Museums & Galleries on Merseyside; Oliver Swann Galleries, Knightsbridge; J.J. Smith, BEM, Cromer; Jack Sharpe RNLI Holyhead; Graeme Somner, Christchurch (World Ship Society); Janet Tierney, Curator, Wellholme Galleries, South Humberside; David Topliss, Curator, National Maritime Museum; Capt P.L. Toghill, Ramsgate; H.F. and E.A. Thompson, Gunnislake, Cornwall; Peter White, Wotton-under-Edge (World Ship Society); all at Poole RNLI; all at David & Charles; Guernsey Press, St Peter Port, Guernsey; Union Transport; and special thanks to Edward, Fiona and their family.

From the outset of this project, my family have been steadfast in their support, researching, typing and reading extracts for me whilst I painted. I am forever grateful to them for understanding my non-participation on so many family occasions over the last three years.

TIM THOMPSON

Many people have helped in the research for and preparation of this book. Special thanks must go to Barry Cox, the RNLI honorary librarian; Simon Stevens of the National Maritime Museum; my colleagues in the RNLI PR department, especially Shelley Woodroffe; Tim Thompson himself for the fruits of his own extensive research; my colleagues in the data processing department for loan of and lessons in operating the lap-top Tosh; and finally Fiona, Thomas and Eleanor for putting up with me working at home.

EDWARD WAKE-WALKER

INDEX

Page numbers in *italic* indicate illustration

Abeille 10, Tug, 74
Ace, Bowman Thomas, 66
Active, Pilot Cutter, 30, *31*
Admiral Berkeley, Transport Ship, 14, *15, 16*
Adventure, Shipwreck, 10
Aldeburgh Lifeboat, 38
Alice, Vessel, *21*
Almondine, Trawler, 61
Ark Royal, HMS, 74

Bailey, Crew Member Dennis (Jnr), 83, *83*
Bailey, Second Coxswain Dennis, 83, *83*
Ballycotton Lifeboat Crew, *56*
Ballyquintin, Co Down, 62
Bee, Gig, 30, *31*
Beeching, James, 11
Bencroy Steamer, 42
Bevan, Superintendent Coxswain Brian, 80, *82*
Blewett, Emergency Mechanic John, 91
Blogg, Coxswain Henry, 8, 12, 50, *52, 53*
Bonita, Ecuadorian Cargo Ship, 84, *84, 85*
Bonnard, Steam Ship, 74
Bougourd, Second Coxswain Peter, 86
Bower, Motor Mechanic Stephen, 77
Bower, Second Coxswain Keith, 77, *78*
Boyle, Coxswain John, 4
Bradford, Lifeboat, 38, *38, 39*
Brazen, HMS, 17
Briton, Gig, 30, *31*
Brockman, Assistant Mechanic Nigel, 91
Bronxville, Steam Ship, *62*
Browning, Steam Ship, 62, *62*
Brownlee, Second Coxswain James, 49
Burton, Captain H.E., Royal Engineers, 46

Charlottenburg, Motor Vessel, 84
Chebogue, Frigate, 9, 64, *65*
Cheeseman, Lt, 14
City of Bradford II, Lifeboat, 58, *59, 60*
City of Bradford IV, Lifeboat, 80, *81, 82*
Claire, Brig, 6
Collins, Captain John, 28
Crewe Trust, 10
Croix, De St Brothers, Francis, Jean and Philip, 18, *19*
Cross, Assistant Mechanic Samuel, 58, *58*
Cross, Coxswain Robert, 58, *58*

Daunt Rock, Lightship, 54, *55*
Davies, Acting Second Coxswain William, 53
Davies, Captain George, 33
Davies, Motor Mechanic William, 66
Denning, Captain, 14
Destouches, Captain, 18
Duke of Northumberland, Lifeboat, 42, *42, 43,*
*   44, 45*

Earner, Tug, 64
Edmund and Mary Robinson, Lifeboat, 70, *71, 72*
Edward Bridges (Civil Service No. 37), Lifeboat, 77, *79*
Edward Prince of Wales, Lifeboat, 64, *65, 66*
Eglon, Second Coxswain Richard,
Else, Lt John, RN, *20*
Engadine, Royal Fleet Auxiliary Vessel, 77
Euphrosyne Kendal, Lifeboat, 74, *76*
Eurofreighter, 77
Evans, Coxswain Richard, 8, 12, 70, *70, 73*

Fanny, Yacht, 18
Fernebo, Steam Ship, 50, *50, 51*
Festing, Lt, *15*
Fidra, Steam Ship, *63*
Fish, Coxswain Charles, 38, *41*
Formby, Lancashire, 10, 27
Forward, Cdr Thomas, 33
Fremantle, Cdr Charles, RN, *1, 4*

Gammon, Coxswain William, 9, 64, *64*
Georgia, Oil Tanker, 52
Godfrey, Thomas, 14
Good Intent, Pilot Boat No. 1, Liverpool, *27*
Grandy, Samuel, 14
Greathead, Henry, 11
Greenhaugh, Crew Member Charles, 91
Grey, James, *30,* 32
Gurth, Trawler, 58, *59, 60*

Hall, Commander Basil, Inspector of Lifeboats, 48, 53
Harold, Steamer, 42, *42, 43, 44*
Hearts of Oak, Lifeboat, 67, *68, 69*
Henry Vernon, Lifeboat, 48, *49*
Hillary, Sir William, 10, 18, *23,* 23, 42
Hindlea, Coaster, 8, 34, 70, *71, 72, 73*
Holy Island, Northumberland, 92
Hood, Bowman William, *58*
Hoopell, Crew Member Sam, *58*
Hunkin, Assistant Mechanic John, 78
Hyperion, HMS, 22

Indian Chief, Merchant Ship, 12, 38, *39*
Isolda, Irish Lights Vessel, 56

James, Lt Horatio, RN, 22
Jeans, Capt, 28
Jenkinson, Second Coxswain W.R., *58*
Jobson, Lt Christopher, RN, 21
Johan Collett, Merchant Ship, 9, 74, *75*
John and Jessie, Sloop, 92, *92*
John Fielden, Lifeboat, 46, *47, 48, 49*
Jones, Hugh, Shore Helper, Moelfre Lifeboat Station, 70
Jordan, Crew Member Peter, 83, *83*
Joy, McGeorge, Master of Revenue Cutter, 92
Julia Park Barry of Glasgow, Lifeboat, 63, *63*

K.T.J.S., Lifeboat, *2,* 4
Kaupanger, Steam Ship, 74
Kent, Duchess of, *73*
Kent, Duke of, *83*
King, Coxswain Thomas, 67, *67*

L.P. and St Helen, Lifeboat, *62*
La Constance, Lugger, 22
Langlands, Coxswain Thomas, 46, *48*
Lewis, Richard, Secretary of RNLI, 12
Lifeboat, The, Journal of the RNLI, 10, *10,* 42, 46, 88
London, Lord Mayor of, 11
Louisa Heartwell, Lifeboat, 50, *50, 51*
Lukin, Lionel, 10
Lyrma, Cargo Vessel, 77, *79*

Madron, Second Coxswain/Mechanic James, 91
Mahony, Robert H., Ballycotton Station Honorary
    Secretary, 54
Major, Motor Mechanic John, 58
Manby Line Throwing Apparatus, 21
Mary Stanford, Lifeboat, 54, *55, 57*
Maurice Georges, Yacht, 67, *69*
McLean, Coxswain John, 63
Mona's Isle, Steamer, 23
Murphy, Coxswain Patrick, 62

Nafsiporos, Freighter, 73
New Commercial, Brig, 33, *33*
Northumberland, Fourth Duke of, 11

Original, The, Lifeboat, 11
Owen, Coxswain William, 42, *43*
Owens, Motor Mechanic, 73

Palling Lifeboat Station, 52
Pattimore, Motor Mechanic Eric, 74
Peake, Thomas, 14
Peake, James, 12
Penlee, Cornwall, 12
Peterhead, Aberdeenshire, 63
Petit, Coxswain Hubert, 9, 74, *74*
Petit, Crew Member John, 74
Plenty, Pellew Lifeboat, 30
Polkerris, Cornwall, 20
Poplar Lifeboat Depot, *12*
Pratten, Lieutenant John, RN, 22
President Kruger, Frigate, 74, *75*
Providence, Fishing Vessel, 20
Pyrin, Steamer, 50

Revi, Cargo Vessel, 80, *81*
Richards, Mrs Mary, *87*
Richards, Coxswain Trevelyan, 9, 88, *88*
Robinson, Lt Robert, 23

Rodgers, Joseph (also known as Joie Rodriguez), *34,*
    36, 70
Rohilla, Hospital Ship, 12, 46, *47*
Rollinson, Crew Member Sydney, 83, *83*
Roscius, Passenger Ship, 28, *29*
Royal Charter, Passenger Ship, 8, 12, 34, *35,* 37, 70
Runswick, Steamer, 63, *63*

Saltwick, Steamer, 63, *63*
Samtampa, Steamer, 64
Sayers, Assistant Mechanic Ronald, 83, *83*
Sayers, Motor Mechanic Barry, 83, *83*
Scales, Coxswain Michael, 84, *87*
Scarborough Lifeboat Station, 64
Scotia, 28, *28, 29*
Sir William Arnold, Lifeboat, 84, *85, 86, 87*
Sliney, Coxswain Patrick, 54, *54, 57*
Sliney, William, *54*
Smith, Coxswain Robert, 46, *48*
Smith, Crew Member Kevin, 91
Solomon Browne, Lifeboat, 88, *89,* 90
Sound Fisher, Steamer, 42
Spurn Head, *61, 80*
Steel, Captain Charles RN, 30
St George, Steamer, 23
St Helier, Jersey, 18, 67
St Mary's, Isles of Scilly, 30
Stolwijk, Steamer, *2,* 4
Stone, R.F., Esq., QC, 91
Storey, Crew Member Michael, 83, *83*
Sumner, Richard, 27, *27*
Sylvia, Revenue Cutter, 33, *33*
Symmes, Lt Henry RN, 6

Tenedos, HMS, Royal Naval Destroyer, 56
Thames, Steam Packet, 30, *30, 31*
Thomas, Gig, 30, *31*
Titanic, SS, 46
Torrible, James, 14
Torrie, Crew Member Barry, 91
Tower of Refuge, Douglas, *26*
True Blue, Lifeboat, 24, *25*
Tyne Class Lifeboat, *11*

Union Star, Coaster, 9, 88, *88, 89, 90, 91*

Vondy, Coxswain Isaac, 23, *26*
Vulcan, Paddle Steamer, 38, *39*

Wales, HRH Prince of, later King George V, 44, *52*
Walker, Lt, *15*
Wallis, Crew Member Gary, 91
Willis, Capt G.W., RN, 17
Wilson Thomas, MP, 14, 18
Wouldhave, William, 11

96